Wilderness Navigation Handbook

D1366599

Artistic illustrations: Anne Price

Technical illustrations: Fred Touche

Warning

Be aware that navigation is only one part of whatever wilderness activity you choose to engage in. Your chosen activity is likely to be dangerous and carry significant risk of personal injury or death and should only be undertaken with a full understanding of all the inherent risks. In addition, poor implementation of navigation techniques may augment the inherent risks associated with your chosen activity.

There are no guaranties, either expressed or implied, that this book contains accurate or complete information. Your most important navigation tool is your brain. Before using any information from this book, make sure this information makes sense. The author accepts no responsibility for your lack of judgment.

National Library of Canada Cataloguing in Publication

Touche, Fred, 1954-
   Wilderness navigation / Fred Touche ; Anne Price, illustrator.
   Second printing, 2005

Includes index.
ISBN-13: 978-0-9732527-0-5
ISBN-10: 0-9732527-0-7

   1. Orienteering—Equipment and supplies. 2. Navigation—Equipment and supplies. I. Price, Anne, 1980- II. Title.

   GV200.5.T68 2004   796.58   C2004-901366-1

Comments on this book

For questions or comments regarding the content of this book, or to order additional copies, email author at: FredT@Bluesoft.ca

Cover design by Abacus Graphics – Oceanside, California

Printed in Canada by Friesens Corporation

Printed on 20% post-consumer waste paper.

Table of Contents

Table of Contents

Table of Contents

Foreword

The idea for this book started innocently just before the turn of the millennium. There were certain facts about navigation that had puzzled me for years, but for some reason could not find clear explanations to. A frustrating search led to long hours in libraries and surfing the web where I eventually managed, piece-by-piece, to get some of the information that I wanted. "If only all this stuff was in one place" was a thought that led to the next idea: "why don't I write a book about navigation."

Having roamed around the wilderness since childhood, navigation and wilderness was a natural match. How could I go wrong with my newfound theoretical knowledge combined with years of unforgiving practical experience? As the millennium rolled around, I made a resolution to go ahead with the book. After an ambitious start, the project soon bogged down with unexpected difficulties. The book was continually morphing into a new creature that could not be tamed, and there were of course other things to do that were more fun.

Although at times painfully slow, progress never completely ground to a halt. After three years, there were things that looked like chapters of incomplete information. Realizing that nothing less than an all out push was going to finish off the project, I started working on the book full time. The book was finally completed four years after its conception. The result is hopefully something that you will find useful during your journeys of exploration.

Fred Touche

March 2004

Acknowledgments

After the initial draft of this book was completed, I asked several avid outdoor enthusiasts if they could review the material. Some were hesitant, while others were eager to help. I would like to thank all those who did sacrifice their valuable time to get involved in this project. Their contribution has been invaluable in making the Wilderness Navigation Handbook an authoritative text.

The first to get involved was Verena Shaw, who proofread the initial draft and did a great job straightening out the many spelling and grammatical errors. A concurrent technical review of the material was done by Paul Kubik and John Hebron who suggested several important changes to the subject matter. John, with his PhD in physics, seemed to take pleasure in debunking several of my key assumptions, particularly regarding astronomy and magnetism. A general review of the content was carried out by Don Funk and James Ram, who discovered yet more grammatical blunders and several vague passages that needed clarification. Jim Mandelli, an expert navigator with more than 30 adventure races under his belt, came onboard late in the game. His knowledge of the practical aspects of land navigation was indispensable. Christine Matterson performed an excellent, thorough final edit before the book was sent off to the printing presses.

I would like to acknowledge all those who helped with the assembly of the book. One of my most intractable problems was how to draw three-dimensional illustrations. Fortunately, Soegi Hartano, a computer aided drafting specialist, came to my rescue, effortlessly tutoring me on the nuances of computer graphics. Annika Lindberg and Wendy Johnstone assisted with the layout of the book, and Robert Dynowski helped with the cover design.

I wish to extend a special thanks to Anne Price for her artistic illustrations that have undoubtedly made a generally dry topic more fun to read, and to my parents for their financial support that has made the publication of this book possible. I am also grateful for the help that I received from many strangers during the long research phase, most who will never know that their expertise went into this book.

Introduction

Navigation is both an art and a science, requiring creativity as well as raw technical skills. It has always been an intricate part of human activity. In the past our very survival may have hinged on using natural navigation clues to find a decent food source and then retrace the route back to the cave. In stark contrast, present-day navigation systems can guide an aircraft across oceans and continents to a perfect landing in zero visibility. Future space travelers will no doubt use devices that are even more sophisticated. Despite these technological advancements, we often find ourselves frustrated by navigational tasks. Just ask anyone who has tried to find his or her way out of an unfamiliar city.

Studies have shown that having a general sense of direction is closely linked to the ability to mentally rotate objects. This may explain why some people easily become disoriented while others have seemingly no trouble finding their way. The widespread belief that some people, especially members of indigenous groups, can navigate purely by instinct is however a myth. Wherever you are on Earth, you are likely surrounded by clues that you can use for navigation. It isn't so much an innate sense of direction that differentiates navigators, but rather the ability to recognize navigational clues and put them to effective use.

The introduction of the global positioning system (GPS) and the availability of low-cost GPS receivers has revolutionized navigation. Travel during poor visibility and through terrain devoid of landmarks can easily be done by anyone willing to put their trust in instruments. Then again, overreliance on technology is also a sure way to get into trouble. High-tech gadgets have a tendency to fail at the worst possible moment, and you may suddenly find yourself navigating like your ancestors.

Except for a chapter on emergency communication, this book is strictly about navigation. It does not deal with wilderness survival, route finding, or the sport of orienteering. The aim is to take away the mystique of navigation by explaining all the essential tools and techniques. If you are a raw beginner, concentrate on learning how to navigate with a map, compass, altimeter, and GPS receiver before diving into topics such as celestial navigation. If you are already a competent navigator, this book will almost certainly give you a deeper understanding of how things work, and more importantly, why things sometimes don't work.

An earnest attempt was made to present the material in logical order and avoid disruptive references to previous or subsequent sections. Unfortunately, this had to balanced with keeping distinct topics together, and avoiding excessive repetition. No attempt has been made to separate basic from advanced topics. If you get bogged down, skip to the next section and return later to the material that you found challenging.

This book is dedicated to the memory
of John Millar and Guy Edwards who
never returned from the wilderness

Chapter 1
Maps

Maps use patterns, colors, and symbols to describe a portion of Earth's surface. Maps are never exact, nor complete, representations of the real world. Different types of maps provide different kinds of information. For example, a road map may show cities, roads, and highways while ignoring terrain features such as valleys or mountain ranges. For off road navigation, topographic maps that use contour lines to describe the shape of the terrain are superior to other types of maps. For ocean and coastal navigation, nautical charts that show the shape of the underwater topography are the preferred choice.

When selecting a map, make sure that it includes the following: (1) legend, (2) scale, (3) contour interval, (4) grid lines, and (5) declination diagram. The legend tells you the meaning of the symbols, lines, and colors on the map. The scale and contour interval allow you to calculate distances, elevations, and slopes from the map. Grid lines make it easier to pinpoint a position on the map. The declination diagram shows you how to adjust your compass to compensate for Earth's irregular magnetic field.

1.1 Legend

The map legend shows the meaning of the colors and symbols on your map. Unfortunately, there is no worldwide standard so the colors and symbols may mean different things on different maps. This is why it is important to consult the legend before using a map from an unfamiliar series.

Colors

Since there are only a few colors to choose from, colors normally show entities that cover significant portions of the map. For example, vegetation zones are shown in green, bodies of water in blue, glaciers in white, urban areas in red, and areas with little or no vegetation in brown.

Symbols

Map symbols are graphic representations of natural and man-made features. Point features such as campsites, lighthouses, or survey markers are shown as single symbols. Linear features such as roads, trails, power lines, railway tracks, rivers, or political boundaries are shown as dashed or continuous lines. Areas such as swamps, moraines, tidal flats, or sand dunes are shown as groups of identical symbols. Symbols are almost always shown at an exaggerated scale. Otherwise, they would be too small to be visible on the map.

Example of symbols

Point features		Linear features		Area features	
Tower	⊙	Highway	══════	Moraine	∷∴∵∷∴
Lighthouse	☼	Railway	┼─┼─┼─┼	Coral reef	˙˷ϟ!ˑ
Bridge	≍	Powerline	▪┄┄▪┄┄▪	Lake	▬▬
Building	▰	Trail	─ ─ ─ ─	Swamp	⸱⸱⸱⸱
Campsite	▲	Boundary	▬▬▬▬▬	Tidal flat	⋰⋰⋰
Survey marker	△	River	～～～	Mangroves	🌿🌿🌿

1.2 Scale

All maps or charts are drawn to a specific scale. The scale is the relationship between a distance on the map versus the same distance in the real world. A large-scale map shows a small area in great detail, while a small-scale map covers a large area but with little detail. Selecting a map with an appropriate scale is therefore a compromise between coverage and detail, and depends on your intended activity. For example, climbing a mountain with complex topography requires a large-scale map, while a small-scale map may be a better choice for a long canoe trip. The scale that you see written on the map is just an approximation. It is never completely constant across the whole map, but varies according to the projection that was used to create the map. The larger the area that a map covers, the more susceptible it is to scale variations. The scale can be expressed as a verbal scale, a ratio scale, or a bar scale.

Verbal scale

A verbal scale uses words to express the relationship between a distance on the map and the corresponding distance in the real world.

Example of verbal scale

The following is written in the margins of your map: "4 cm on the map represents 1 km on the ground." Here it is implied that a distance of 4 centimeters on the map is equal to 1 kilometer in the real world. This relationship allows you to calculate any other real world distance from the map. For example, a measured distance of 15.6 cm on the map represents (15.6 cm)/(4 cm) x 1 km = 3.9 km in the real world.

Ratio scale

The scale of a map can be expressed as a ratio between a distance on the map versus the same distance in the real world. Some people find ratio scales confusing because distances are not tied to a specific unit. You can use any unit you want as long as you stick to the same unit during the conversion between map and real world distances. After doing the conversion, you can of course convert the resulting distance into other units.

Example of ratio scale

A map with "Scale 1:50 000" written in the margins means that the distance between any two points is 50 000 times longer in the real world than on the map. For example, a distance of 8.5 cm on the map would be 50 000 x 8.5 cm = 425 000 cm = 4250 m = 4.25 km in the real world.

Bar scale

A bar scale shows real world distances directly on the map. Bar scales are the most common type of scale, and are easy to understand because of their graphical nature. A common practice is to show several bar scales on the same map, each representing a different length unit. Bar scales are often shown together with ratio or verbal scales.

Examples of bar scales

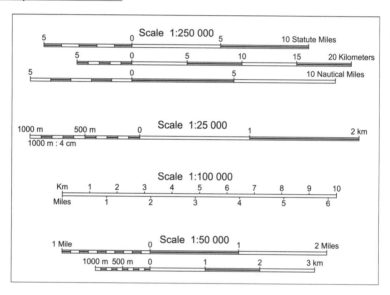

1.3 How to measure distances on a map

To calculate the real world distance of a proposed route, you must first measure the corresponding distance on the map. This is easy if the route is a straight line between two points. Simply measure the distance with a ruler. If you don't have a ruler, keep in mind that orienteering compasses often have rulers inscribed in their base plates. Another method is to use the grid lines that are drawn across some maps as a measuring device. The grid lines form an array of identical squares with sides of a specific length. After figuring out the dimensions of one square, the grid effectively becomes a ruler. For more complicated routes, break up your route into straight-line segments and measure the distance of each segment separately. Add the lengths of all the segments to calculate the total length of the route.

To measure a curved path, lay out a string along the route. Pinch the string with your fingers at the two end points of the route and then pull the string tight. Place the string along a ruler, or across grid squares, and read off the distance. If your map has a bar scale, place the string on the bar scale and directly read off the real world distance. Instead of a string, you can use a map wheel, also known as a curvimeter. Set the counter to zero and then roll the wheel along your route. The curvimeter will display the accumulated distance. Pay attention to the units. Curvimeters can either directly display real world distances for maps of certain scales, or just show the actual distance on the map. In the latter case, you must convert the map distance to the real world distance.

If you have access to digital maps and related software, a computer will calculate and display the distance of your route. A typical software package lets you create a route by clicking on your start point, end point, and any intermediate points. The program displays the cumulative distance between all the adjacent points. Some software packages allow you to trace curved routes on the digital map. This makes your calculated distance even more accurate.

1.4 Geographic coordinate system

The geographic coordinate system is one of the two widely used methods for pinpointing locations on a map. It covers Earth's entire surface. A location is identified by specifying its latitude (parallel) and longitude (meridian). Latitudes and longitudes can be visualized as an array of imaginary lines running along Earth's surface. A position is measured in angle units: degrees (°), minutes of arc ('), and seconds of arc ("). Each degree is subdivided into 60 minutes of arc, which in turn are subdivided into 60 seconds of arc. Sometimes decimal degrees are used instead of minutes and seconds of arc, or decimal minutes instead of seconds of arc. For example, $156°16'21" = 156°16.35' = 156.2725°$.

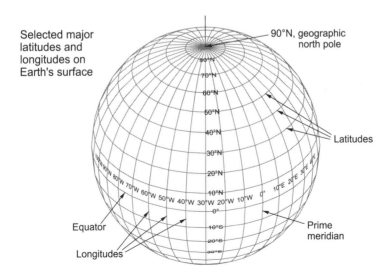

Selected major latitudes and longitudes on Earth's surface

90°N, geographic north pole

Latitudes

Equator

Prime meridian

Longitudes

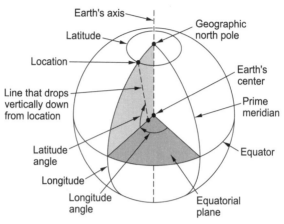

How latitudes and longitudes are derived

Latitude

The latitude of a location is defined as the angle between the equatorial plane and an imaginary line that drops vertically down from the location. This line generally does not intersect the equatorial plane exactly at Earth's center because Earth's surface is slightly flattened at the poles. The latitude is a measure of how far north or south a location is from the equator. Latitudes can be visualized as a series of concentric circles centered on the geographic poles and expanding to a maximum radius at the equator.

To specify the latitude, state the latitude angle and whether the location is north (N) or south (S) of the equator. The latitude is 90°N at the north pole, 0° at the equator, and 90°S at the south pole. Other locations have intermediate latitudes, for example, 46°25'09"S. The length along Earth's surface of one minute of latitude is proportional to the radius of curvature along the local surface; it varies from 1843 m at the equator to 1862 m at the poles. The original definition of the nautical mile was the average distance of one minute of arc of latitude along Earth's surface. Today, the nautical mile is defined as precisely 1852 m.

Longitude

The longitude of a location is defined as the angle, parallel to the equatorial plane, between the location and a reference longitude called the prime meridian. By convention, the prime meridian (0°) is the longitude that runs through an established point at Greenwich, England. From there, other longitudes increase eastward and westward until they meet at 180° on the opposite side of Earth. The longitude is thus a measure of how far east (E) or west (W) a location is from the prime meridian.

Longitudes can be visualized as a series of north-south lines that converge at the poles. To specify the longitude, state the longitude angle and whether the location is east or west of the prime meridian, for example, 105°57'15"E. The length along Earth's surface of one minute of longitude varies from 1855 m at the equator to 0 at the geographic poles.

1.4.1 Geographic coordinates on maps

Major latitudes and longitudes are shown as lines across the map or as tick marks in the margins. On most maps or charts, only selected latitudes and longitudes are completely labeled. To prevent clutter, other lines are labeled with partial numbers. For example, only the minutes of arc are shown. The standard way to describe a location with geographic coordinate is to state the latitude followed by the longitude. For example, 46°25'09"S, 105°57'15"E.

For a rough approximation of the latitude and longitude of a location on a map, look at the nearest latitude and longitude lines that surround the location. Visually estimate where the location is relative to the nearest latitude and longitude lines. Take into account that there are 60 minutes of arc in each degree and 60 seconds of arc in each minute of arc.

For more precise results, use a ruler to measure the distance between the location and the nearest lower latitude line, and then measure the distance between the nearest higher and lower latitude lines. Divide the first distance by the second distance to obtain the proportional distance. Convert the proportional distance into angle units and then add the result to the nearest lower latitude line. Calculate the longitude in a similar manner.

<u>Example of how to determine geographic coordinates on a map</u>

On the map below, the proportional distance between Location A and the nearest lower latitude line is 17 mm/38 mm = 0.45. The angular distance between the longitude lines on the map is 1' = 60". Converting from proportional distance to angular units gives 0.45 x 60" = 27". Adding this result to the nearest lower latitude line gives 53°01'00"N + 27" = 53°01'27"N.

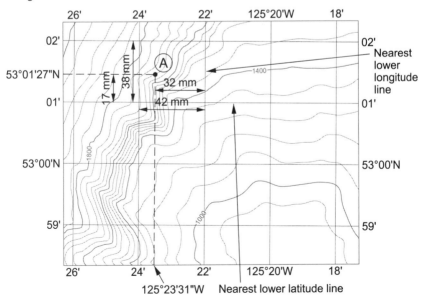

The proportional distance between Location A and the nearest lower longitude line is 32 mm/42 mm = 0.76. The angular distance between longitude lines is 2' = 2 x 60" = 120". Converting the proportional distance into angle units gives 0.76 x 120" = 91" = 1'31". Adding this result to the nearest lower longitude line gives 125°22'00"W + 1'31" = 125°23'31"W. The complete geographic position is written as 53°01'27"N, 125°23'31"W.

Similar types of calculations can be done to solve the reverse problem where you already have a written position and want to pinpoint it on the map. The above example clearly illustrates the trouble you have to go through to accurately determine a location with geographic coordinates. The task is even more difficult on maps where the latitude or longitude lines aren't straight.

1.5 Map projections

Projections are mathematical methods that are used to transfer geographic information from Earth's surface to maps. It is impossible to represent any portion of Earth's curved surface on a flat map without some kind of distortion of scale, direction, shape, or distance. The type of projection governs the type of distortion. Reducing one type of distortion will inevitably increase another type. Mapmakers are forced to compromise by deciding what sort of distortion is acceptable. This is largely determined by the intended use of the map.

Projections can be visualized as one or more light sources shining rays through Earth's surface onto a projection surface that may be partially located inside Earth. The rays produce an image of the topography and geographic coordinates on the projection surface. In areas where the projection surface is inside Earth, the image is formed by rays bouncing back from Earth's surface along the same path. The shape and location of the projection surface and the location(s) of the light source(s) define the type of projection. A map or chart is simply a portion of the projection surface.

The scale is always correct where the projection surface touches or cuts into Earth's surface. Features are shown too small where the projection surface is inside Earth and too

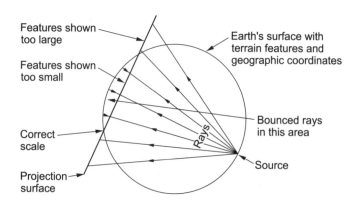

large where the projection surface is outside Earth. Distances may be correct from one point to all other points, or from certain points to certain other points, but never from all points to all others points. In most cases, directions (bearings) do not follow straight lines. On large-scale maps, the distortion is usually minimal and can be safely ignored. Many types of projections exist, but only four widely used types are discussed here.

1.5.1 Mercator projection

In the Mercator projection, Earth's surface is projected onto a cylinder wrapped around the equator. A series of light sources are located along Earth's axis of rotation, with each source striking a particular portion of the projection surface.

The scale is correct only along the equator. Features are shown increasingly too large as you move away from the equator, becoming infinite at the poles. Shapes of small features are correct throughout the projection surface. Distances are correct only along the equator. Straight lines on the map have constant bearings but are generally not the shortest distance between two points.

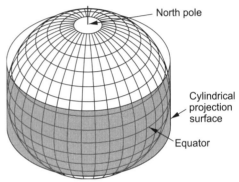

North pole

Cylindrical projection surface

Equator

The Mercator projection is not used for polar regions because of the extreme distortion of scale and shape of large features at high latitudes. It is a popular projection for ocean charts because a route that follows a constant bearing is always a straight line on the chart.

1.5.2 Lambert conformal conic projection

With the Lambert conformal conic projection, Earth's surface is projected onto a cone oriented with its apex over one of the geographic poles. The cone cuts through Earth along two latitudes called the standard parallels. The source is located along Earth's axis.

The scale is correct along the two standard parallels. Features between the standard parallels are shown too small, while features outside the standard parallels are shown increasingly too large. Shapes of small features are correct throughout the projection surface. Distances are correct only along the standard parallels. Bearings are correct only along the longitudes.

The Lambert conformal conic projection is well suited for maps with large east-west coverage and is used for some polar maps.

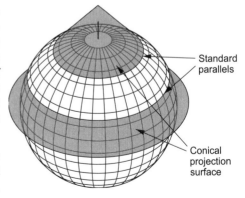

Standard parallels

Conical projection surface

1.5.3 Universal transverse Mercator projection

The universal transverse Mercator (UTM) projection is complicated. The projection surface is a cylinder wrapped around Earth's poles along a longitude called the central meridian. The cylinder diameter is slightly smaller than Earth's diameter and cuts through Earth's surface along two lines parallel to the central meridian called secant lines. The light source is a series of points along Earth's axis of rotation. Only a narrow north-south strip, 3° of longitude on either side of the central meridian, is projected. For global coverage, the cylinder is twisted by 6° increments, creating an array of 60 different projection strips, each 6° of longitude wide.

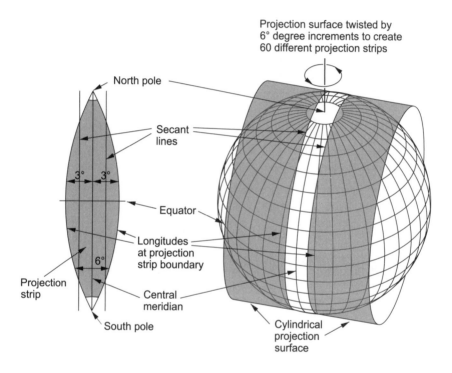

The scale is correct only along the two secant lines. Features between the two secant lines are shown too small, while features outside the secant lines are shown increasingly too large. Shapes of small features are correct throughout the projection surface. Distances are correct only along the secant lines. Distortion of distance, direction, and shapes of large features increases as you move away from the central meridian. Straight lines on the map do not have constant bearings except along the central meridian.

The UTM projection is used in conjunction with the UTM grid and is well suited for maps with large north-south coverage. It is a favorite choice for large and medium scale topographic maps everywhere in the world except in polar regions.

1.5.4 Polar stereographic projection

The polar stereographic projection is one of the simplest types of projection. The projection surface is a flat plane that is centered on one of the geographic poles and cuts into Earth along a latitude called the standard parallel. The source is located at the opposite geographic pole.

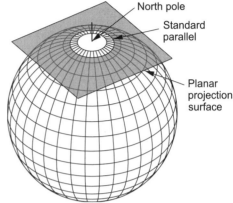

The scale is correct along the standard parallel. Features are shown too small at latitudes inside the standard parallel and increasingly too large outside the standard parallel. Shapes of small features are correct throughout the projection surface but the shape distortion of large features increases as you move away from the pole. Distances are correct only along the standard parallel, and bearings are correct only along the longitudes.

The polar stereographic projection is used mainly for topographic maps in polar regions in conjunction with the universal polar stereographic (UPS) grid.

1.6 UTM grid

A grid consists of an array of parallel and perpendicular lines drawn on the map. Each grid line is labeled with a number that is equal to the line's real-world distance from a specific line of origin. The distance units vary depending on the grid. Unlike latitude and longitude lines, grid lines are not distorted on the map because the grid lines are drawn on the projection surface after the projection has been completed. Grid lines form an array of identical squares, making them well-suited for finding positions on a map.

Many nations and organizations have developed grids that cover selected parts of Earth's surface. The universal transverse Mercator (UTM) grid is the most widely used grid in the world. It is tied to the universal transverse Mercator projection and covers Earth's entire surface between 80°S and 84°N. This book only deals with the UTM and the associated UPS grid. Other grids are based on similar principles and are usually simpler.

1.6.1 UTM zones

In the UTM grid, the nonpolar surface of Earth is divided into 60 vertical bands that coincide with the projection strips derived from the UTM projection. All the vertical bands are 6° of longitude wide. They are numbered from west to east, beginning with Band 1 (180°W - 174°W) and ending with Band 60 (174°E - 180°E).

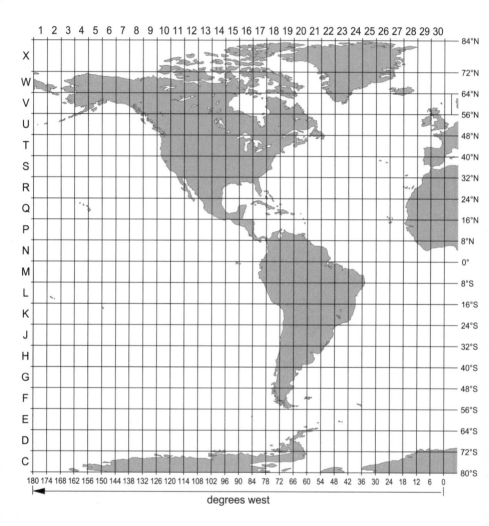

UTM zones - western hemisphere

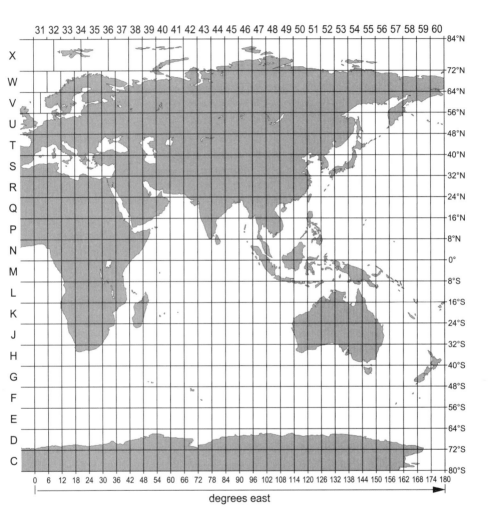

UTM zones - eastern hemisphere

The UTM grid also uses 20 horizontal bands that are generally 8° high. The horizontal bands are lettered from south to north beginning with Band C (80°S - 72°S) and ending with Band X (72°N - 84°N). The letters "I" and "O" have been omitted in order to eliminate confusion with the numbers "1" and "0". A UTM zone is the overlap between a vertical and a horizontal band. With the exception of the special UTM zones, each zone is 6° of longitude wide by 8° of latitude high (see maps of UTM zones on previous pages).

Examples of UTM zone boundaries

Zone 10U, located in the northern hemisphere, is bounded by latitudes 48°N and 56°N, and longitudes 120°W and 126°W. Zone 37L, located in the southern hemisphere, is bounded by latitudes 8°S and 16°S, and longitudes 36°E and 42°E.

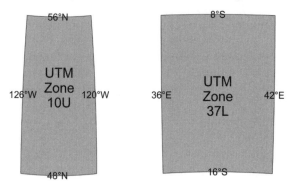

Both zones have the same "height" because adjacent latitudes are very nearly the same distance apart. Zone 10U is narrower than Zone 37L because it is located further from the equator.

Special UTM zones

The UTM grid is not completely consistent and is afflicted by a few exemptions called special UTM zones:

- Band X, the northernmost horizontal band, has been extended northward by 4°. Each zone in this band is 12° of latitude high instead of 8°.

- To accommodate southwest Norway, Zone 32V has been extended westward by 3° at the expense of Zone 31V.

- To accommodate Svalbard, Zone 33X and 35X have been extended both westward and eastward by 3°.

- Zone 31X has been extended eastward by 3° and Zone 37X westward by 3°.

- Zone 32X, 34X, and 36X have been eliminated.

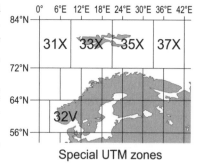

Special UTM zones

1.6.2 Easting and northing in UTM grid

Any nonpolar location on Earth can be identified by specifying its UTM zone, easting, and northing. The easting is a measure of how far east or west the location is from a reference longitude. The northing is a measure of how far north or south the location is from the equator.

The longitude running through the middle of each UTM zone is called the central meridian. It is defined as having an easting of 500 000 m. A point east of the central meridian has an easting of 500 000 m plus its distance in meters from the central meridian along the projection surface. Conversely, a point west of the central meridian has an easting of 500 000 m minus its distance in meters from the central meridian.

A point north of the equator has a northing equal to its distance in meters from the equator along the projection surface. A point south of the equator has a northing of 10 000 000 m minus its distance in meters from the equator.

Examples of how easting and northing are derived in UTM grid

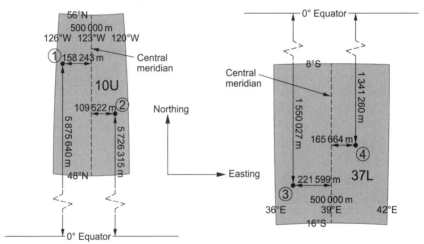

Location 1: Zone 10U
Easting = 500 000 m - 158 243 m = 341 757 m E
Northing = 5 875 640 m N

Location 2: Zone 10U
Easting = 500 000 m + 109 522 m = 609 522 m E
Northing = 5 726 315 m N

Location 3: Zone 37L
Easting = 500 000 m - 221 599 m = 278 401 m E
Northing = 10 000 000 m - 1 550 027 m = 8 449 973 m N

Location 4: Zone 37L
Easting = 500 000 m + 165 664 m = 665 664 m E
Northing = 10 000 000 m - 1 341 260 m = 8 658 740 m N

1.6.3 UTM grid on maps

Each UTM zone is generally large enough to contain many medium or large-scale maps. The zone(s) in which the map is located is normally written somewhere in the margins of the map. The horizontal band label (letters C through X) is sometimes omitted from the zone label because the northing uniquely establishes the horizontal band as long as you know what hemisphere you're in. Major eastings and northings are shown as lines across the map or as tick marks in the margins of the map. On most maps, only selected grid lines are completely labeled. To prevent clutter, other lines are labeled with only partial grid numbers. Although not necessarily aligned parallel to the map edges, UTM grid lines always form an array of perfect squares. This makes them inherently well-suited for pinpointing positions. A UTM grid position is usually stated as the zone followed by the easting and then the northing. For example: Zone 37L, 665 664 m E, 8 658 740 m N.

To find the grid numbers for a location on the map, first figure out the real world distance of the sides of one square. This can be done from the map scale or by looking at any fully labeled grid line. Measure or visually estimate the proportional distance between the location and the nearest lower easting line. Multiply the proportional distance by the real world length of one square. Add this distance to the nearest lower easting line to obtain the easting for the location. Use the same procedure to calculate the northing.

<u>Example of how to estimate easting and northing on a map</u>

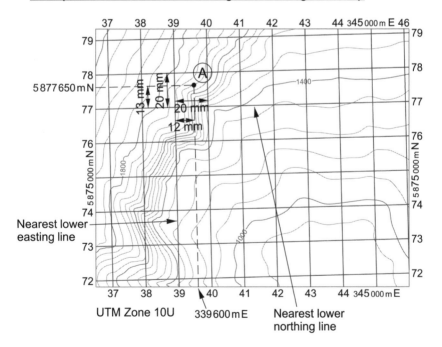

With a ruler, you measure the size of each grid square as 20 mm x 20 mm. By looking at the fully labeled lines 345 000 m E and 5 875 000 m N, you deduce that each square represents 1000 m x 1000 m in the real world. The distance between Location A and the nearest lower easting line (partially labeled as 39) is 12 mm on the map. The proportional distance between Location A and the nearest lower easting line is 12 mm/20 mm = 0.6. Multiplying this by the real world length of one square gives 0.6 x 1000 m = 600 m. Adding this distance to the nearest lower easting line gives an easting of 339 000 m + 600 m = 339 600 m.

The distance between Location A and the nearest lower northing line (partially labeled as 77) is 13 mm on the map. The proportional distance between Location A and the nearest lower easting line is 13 mm/20 mm = 0.65. Multiplying this by the real world length of one square gives 0.65 x 1000 m = 650 m. Adding this distance to the nearest lower northing line gives a northing of 5 877 000 m + 650 m = 5 877 650 m. The complete UTM grid position is stated as: Zone 10U, 339 600 m E, 5 877 650 m N.

Similar types of calculations can be performed to solve the reverse problem where you already have a written UTM position and want to pinpoint it on the map.

1.6.4 Truncated grid numbers

Many hiking and mountaineering guidebooks denote a UTM grid location as a 4, 6, or 8-digit number associated with a certain map. The first half of the digits in the number refers to a truncated easting and the rest of the digits are part of a truncated northing. For example, the first three digits of a 6-digit truncated grid number refer to the easting and the last three digits to the northing. The truncated grid number itself is usually all you need to pinpoint the location on the map. Other times, such as when entering the location into a global positioning system (GPS) receiver, you must expand the truncated grid number into a complete easting and northing. This requires looking at the map and doing some detective work.

Example of how to expand a truncated grid number

Suppose a guidebook tells you that a cabin is located at UTM Grid 781 883 on a particular 1:50 000 scale map. You want to enter this location into your GPS receiver. Your GPS receiver requires a complete easting, which is always a 6-digit number and a complete northing that can be as long as a 7-digit number.

The first three digits, 781, is the truncated easting. Since the map scale is 1:50 000, assume that the author has given you the location of the cabin to the nearest 100 m. Therefore, attach two zeros to the end of the truncated easting to make it 78 100. Now look at your map. If the left side of the map shows an easting of 465 000 while the right side shows 499 000, your easting must be somewhere in between and the first number of your easting must be 4. The complete easting is therefore 478 100 m E.

The last three numbers, 883, is the truncated northing. Add two zeros to make this number 88 300. If the map shows a bottom northing of 5 484 000 and a top northing of 5 510 000, your only logical choice is to add 54 to the front of your northing. The complete northing is therefore 5 488 300 m N.

1.7 UPS grid

The universal polar stereographic (UPS) grid is an extension of the UTM grid. It covers polar areas north of 84°N and south of 80°S. The UPS grid lines are drawn on a projection surface derived from the polar stereographic map projection. On a map, the UPS grid is used in the same manner as the UTM grid.

1.7.1 UPS zones

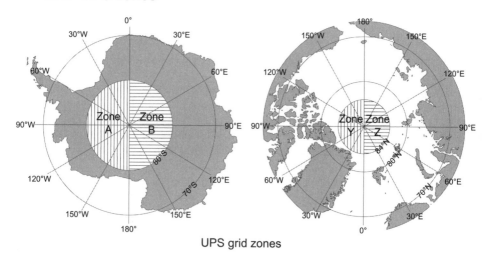

UPS grid zones

There are four half-moon shaped UPS zones, two located by the north pole and two by the south pole. Zone A covers the western hemisphere south of 80°S while Zone B covers the eastern hemisphere south of 80°S. Similarly, Zone Y covers the western hemisphere north of 84°N while Zone Z covers the eastern hemisphere north of 84°N.

1.7.2 Easting and northing in UPS grid

Easting and northing are confusing in the UPS grid, as these terms generally do not correlate with the cardinal directions east and north. This makes UPS positions intuitively difficult to visualize. The easting baseline, along longitudes 0° and 180°, is defined as having an easting of 2 000 000 m. A location in the eastern hemisphere has an easting of 2 000 000 m plus the distance in meters from the easting baseline. A location in the western hemisphere has an easting of 2 000 000 m minus the distance in meters from the easting baseline.

The direction of the northing is awkward to remember. The northing baseline, along longitudes 90°W and 90°E, is defined as having a northing of 2 000 000 m. In the southern hemisphere a location on either side of the 0° longitude has a northing of 2 000 000 m plus the distance in meters from the northing baseline. In the northern hemisphere, that formula applies to a location on either side of the 180° longitude. Conversely, in the southern hemisphere a location on either side of the 180° longitude has a northing of 2 000 000 m minus the distance in meters from the baseline, while in the northern hemisphere that formula applies to a location on either side of the 0° longitude.

Examples of how easting and northing are derived in UPS grid

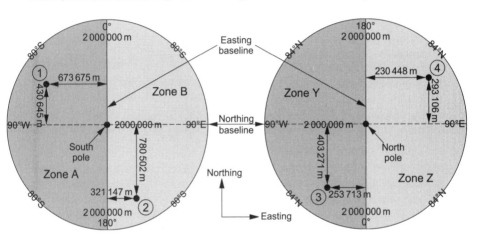

Location 1:   Zone A
Easting = 2 000 000 m - 673 675 m = 1 326 325 m E
Northing = 2 000 000 m + 430 645 m = 2 430 645 m N

Location 2:   Zone B
Easting = 2 000 000 m + 321 147 m = 2 321 147 m E
Northing = 2 000 000 m - 780 502 m = 1 219 498 m N

Location 3:   Zone Y
Easting = 2 000 000 m - 253 713 m = 1 746 287 m E
Northing = 2 000 000 m - 403 271 m = 1 596 729 m N

Location 4:   Zone Z
Easting = 2 000 000 m + 230 448 m = 2 230 448 m E
Northing = 2 000 000 m + 293 106 m = 2 293 106 m N

1.8 Map datums

Map datums determine precisely where the latitude, longitude, and grid lines are drawn on a map. Datums also govern the heights of terrain features.

1.8.1 Earth's shape

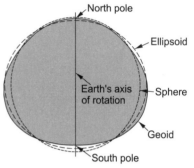

Models of Earth's shape
(shape highly exaggerated)

If Earth were shrunk to the size of a billiard ball, its surface would be almost as smooth as a new billiard ball. The topography of mountain ranges and ocean floors would hardly be noticeable. This doesn't mean that Earth is a perfect sphere. The rotation around its axis generates a centrifugal force that causes the Earth to flatten slightly at the poles and bulge slightly at the equator. A simple geometric shape called an ellipsoid can approximate this shape. The numbers inserted into the ellipsoid formula determine the size of the ellipsoid and how much it bulges, and thus how well it agrees with Earth's real surface. In the past, a new improved global ellipsoid has replaced the old one every few decades or so.

An ellipsoid does not take into account the distortions in shape caused by density variations inside Earth. A complicated model called a geoid has been developed to account for this. A geoid is the surface where gravity is equal. It is derived from measuring Earth's gravity at various locations. A geoid closely approximates the surface to which the oceans would conform if they were free to flow across the continents. It makes Earth look slightly pear-shaped with a slightly larger southern hemisphere and other smaller dips and bulges. New and improved geoid models are continually being developed.

1.8.2 Horizontal datums

Traditionally, ellipsoids have been created to conform only to certain areas of interest. These so-called regional ellipsoids are designed to make a best fit for a specific region while ignoring the rest of Earth's surface. Each regional ellipsoid is associated with a reference point located in the middle of the region. A regional ellipsoid combined with its reference point is called a regional datum. It forms a reference frame from where other positions in the region are computed. Several hundred regional datums are used worldwide.

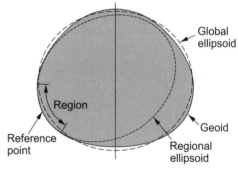

Regional and global ellipsoids
(shape highly exaggerated)

In recent years, the trend has been to use global ellipsoids that cover Earth's entire surface. Global ellipsoids are centered on Earth's center of mass and oriented along Earth's axis of rotation. In general, a global ellipsoid cannot conform to a local area as well as a regional ellipsoid, but has the advantage of worldwide coverage. A global datum consists of a global ellipsoid with positions referenced from the prime meridian and Earth's axis of rotation.

The horizontal datum governs where the latitude, longitude, and grid lines are drawn on the map. Different datums give different geographic coordinates or grid numbers for the same location. Latitude and longitude lines are projected entities while grid lines are drawn onto the map after it has been projected. This means that these two systems are affected differently by datums. When stating the geographic coordinates or grid numbers of a position on a map, always specify the corresponding datum. Using the wrong datum can lead to horizontal position errors of several hundred meters. The horizontal datum is usually written somewhere in the margins of the map.

Example of how datums affect a position

The map below shows geographic coordinate lines from two separate datums, the global 1984 World Geodetic System (WGS 84) and the regional 1927 North American Datum (NAD 27). The NAD 27 latitude lines are 0.6" (19 m) further south than the WGS 84 lines, while the longitude lines are 5.3" (99 m) further west. The geographic coordinate numbers for Location A are shifted in the opposite direction. The latitude is shifted north by 0.6" becoming 53°01'27" + 0.6" = 53°01'27.6"N in NAD 27. The longitude is shifted east by 5.3" becoming 125°23'31" - 5.3" = 125°23'25.7"W.

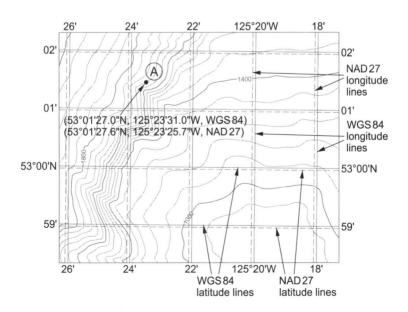

Next, is the same map shown with two sets of UTM grid lines. The NAD 27 easting lines are 95 m further west than the WGS 84 lines, while the northing lines are 203 m further north. The UTM numbers for Location A are shifted in the opposite direction. The easting is shifted east by 95 m becoming 339 600 + 95 = 339 695 m E in NAD 27. The northing is shifted south by 203 m becoming 5 877 650 - 203 = 5 877 447 m N.

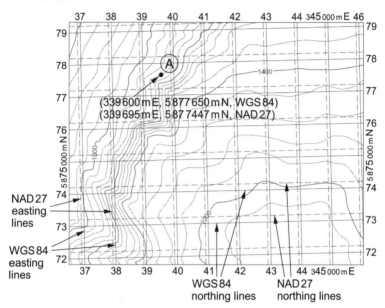

1.8.3 Vertical datums

Map elevations are measured relative to a vertical datum, which is a reference surface that is either an ellipsoid or a geoid. The vertical datum is usually marked somewhere in the margin of the map. The term "mean sea level" that you see on many maps implies that the elevations are relative to a geoid surface. A geoid surface is by definition closely related to the surface that would result if the oceans were free to flow across continents, and essentially coincides with the average water level along a coastline. Away from the

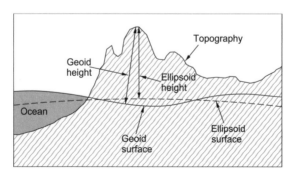

coast, the geoid surface is calculated from measurements of the local gravity. The geoid surface is periodically recalculated leading to changes in surveyed map elevations.

An ellipsoid is sometimes used as a vertical datum. In this case, the surveyed heights on the map are measured relative to the ellipsoid surface instead of mean sea level. Maps can use the same ellipsoid for both the vertical and the horizontal datum but this is rarely the case. Because ellipsoid surfaces are easy to define mathematically, GPS receivers typically calculate elevations relative to an ellipsoid. The elevations are then converted into geoid heights before being displayed on the screen.

1.9 Topographic maps

Topographic maps have two key advantages over other types of maps: (1) they show the shape of the terrain, and (2) allow you to calculate the elevation gain or loss of a proposed route. This makes topographic maps inherently well suited for land navigation. They are also good for finding your way on rivers and small or moderately sized lakes.

1.9.1 Definition of contour lines

Contour lines enable three-dimensional features to be shown on a two-dimensional map. The contour lines are created by joining points of equal elevation. Each contour line therefore represents a specific elevation above sea level. The vertical distance between two adjacent contour lines is called the contour interval. In theory, a map with a small contour interval will always show more detail than a map with a large interval.

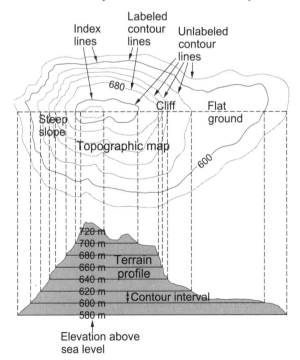

In practice, this is not always the case. If both the map scale and contour interval are small, the map will look like an indistinguishable blob of contour lines.

The horizontal distance between contour lines is inversely proportional to the slope of the terrain. Closely spaced lines indicate steep terrain such as cliffs while sparsely spaced lines reveal gentle slopes.

Usually, every 5th or 10th contour line is drawn in bold print. These bolded lines, called index lines, make it easier to track elevations on the map. Selected contour lines are labeled with their elevations while other lines are left unlabeled.

1.9.2 Finding elevation of unlabeled contour line

Finding the elevation of selected locations along a proposed route enables you to calculate the total elevation gain or loss of the route, which will give you a sense of how strenuous the travel will be. To estimate the elevation of a location, determine the elevation of the nearest contour line. If this contour line is unlabeled, count the number of contour lines to the nearest labeled line. Multiply this number by the contour interval to get the elevation difference. Then add or subtract (whichever is appropriate) the elevation difference to/from the elevation of the labeled line. This yields the elevation of the desired unlabeled contour line.

Elevation of unlabeled line - example

You want to find the elevation the unlabeled contour line on the map shown to the right.

Contour interval = 40 m

Elevation of nearest labeled line = 1800 m

Number lines below labeled line = 4

Elevation difference = 4 x 40 m = 160 m

Elevation of unlabeled line = 1800 - 160 m = 1640 m

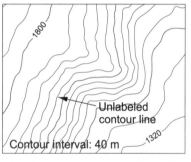

In most real life situations, the location is somewhere between two contour lines. The elevation is therefore somewhere in between the higher and lower contour line.

1.9.3 Calculating slopes

Anytime you're unsure whether a planned route is within your abilities, calculate the angle of the steepest part of the route. This may also help you decide what equipment to bring along. The procedure is straightforward: determine the horizontal distance (run) and the elevation difference (rise) of the slope, and then perform a couple of calculations.

The slope can be represented as a gradient measured in percent, or an angle measured in degrees. The gradient is the ratio between the rise and the run, and is calculated by dividing the rise by the run. The slope angle is calculated by plugging the gradient into a trigonometric function. See Table 1.9 for pre-calculated values.

Slope calculation

1. On the map, use a ruler to measure the run (horizontal distance) of the desired portion of the slope. Measure perpendicular to the contour lines to ensure that the steepest direction of the slope (fall line) is calculated. Multiply the map distance by the scale to get the real world run.

2. Count the number of contour lines along the slope. Multiply the number of contour lines by the contour interval to obtain the rise (elevation difference) of the slope.

3. Divide the rise by the run to get the gradient in decimal units. Multiply the decimal gradient by 100 to obtain the gradient as a percentage.

4. Use Table 1.9 to convert the gradient into degrees. Interpolate for intermediate gradient values.

Table 1.9
Correlation between gradient and slope angle

Gradient	Angle	Gradient	Angle
9%	5°	119%	50°
18%	10°	143%	55°
27%	15°	173%	60°
36%	20°	214%	65°
47%	25°	275%	70°
58%	30°	373%	75°
70%	35°	567%	80°
84%	40°	1143%	85°
100%	45°	Infinite	90°

Example of slope calculation:

You want to calculate the average angle of a particular slope on the map shown below. The scale is 1:50 000 and the contour interval is 40 m.

With a ruler, measure the map run. The result is 14 mm. Multiply the map run by 50 000 to give you the real life run: 14 mm x 50 000 = 700 000 mm = 700 m. The slope covers 6 contour intervals so the rise is 6 x 40 m = 240 m.

The gradient is 240 m/700 m = 0.34 = 100% x 0.34 = 34%. By interpolation, Table 1.9 gives you an average slope angle of around 19°.

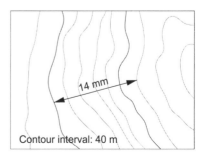

Contour interval: 40 m

Keep in mind that your calculated slope angle is just an average. You will likely encounter steeper as well as flatter sections along that slope. You may be surprised how different the terrain appears in real life than envisioned from looking at the map.

Very few navigators actually calculate the angle of a slope from a topographic map, though it certainly is prudent to do so for off-trail routes through mountainous terrain. Most people just look at the contour lines on the map and judge the slope angle based on experience. Obviously, the only way to get this type of experience is to go outside with your map and check out some real slopes.

1.9.4 How contour lines represent terrain features

Contour lines can represent almost any type of terrain. Although every terrain feature on Earth is in some way different from all others, a particular pattern of contour lines indicates a specific type of feature. Below are some reoccurring types of features, shown with their associated contour line patterns.

Valley

A valley is a long and wide trough that has been carved out by moving glaciers and/or flowing water. If you are at the bottom of a valley, there is higher ground in three directions and lower ground in the other.

On maps, the valley bottom consists of a series of V-shaped or U-shaped contour lines whose closed ends point uphill along the valley floor. V-shaped contour lines indicate a steeper and narrower valley floor than U-shaped lines. Be careful not to confuse a valley with a ridge on the map. Valleys often show a river running along the closed end of the contour lines, which ridges never do.

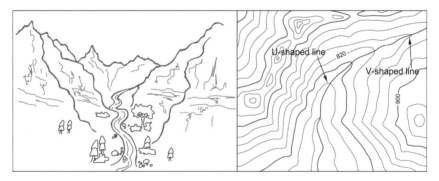

Ridge

A ridge is a linear feature similar to a rooftop. Most mountains have ridges radiating in several directions from the summit. The ridge crest normally undulates or slopes in one direction. On rare occasions, the ridge crest is level.

On maps, a sloped ridge crest consists of V-shaped or U-shaped contour lines with the closed ends pointing downhill. U-shaped lines signify a broad ridge, while V-shaped lines signify a sharp ridge known as an arête. A level ridge crest consists of two parallel contour lines that can be difficult to distinguish from any other parallel lines on the map. There are often bumps and saddles along a ridge, which is one way to differentiate a ridge from a valley or gully.

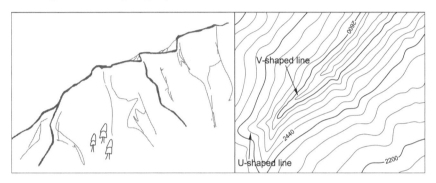

Gully

A gully is a groove running down a slope. Gullies have been gouged out of the slope by running water, avalanches, or rock fall. The contour lines are V-shaped or U-shaped with the closed ends pointing uphill. Inside the gully, there is higher ground in three directions and lower ground in the other. A gully is much smaller and narrower than a valley. A gully located high on a mountain is called a couloir.

Cliff

A cliff is a vertical, near vertical, or overhanging feature. Cliffs are composed of rock that is resistant to erosion. Less resistant rock is often present below a cliff in the form of scree slopes or boulder fields. On maps, the contour lines representing a cliff are very close together and sometimes touch each other. In some cases, the contour lines disappear altogether, making it difficult to determine the slope or height of the cliff.

Pass

A pass is a low point between two areas of higher ground. It can be described as a saddle with higher ground in two opposite directions and lower ground in the other two directions. In many cases, passes are the easiest gateway between two valleys or drainages. On maps, the innermost contour lines of a pass look like an hourglass. A steep and narrow mountain pass is known as a col.

Summit

A summit is a high point surrounded by lower ground in all directions. All mountain massifs and hills contain at least one summit. On maps, the area surrounding the summit has closed contour lines nested inside each other with the high point located inside the innermost contour line. The elevation of the summit is sometimes written on the map.

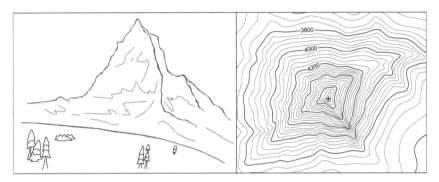

Canyon

A canyon is a trench that has been carved out by flowing water. In general, a canyon is narrower and has much steeper walls than a valley. On maps, a canyon consists of two sets of closely spaced lines, each set representing one of the walls. Smaller canyons sometime branch out from the main one. Depending on the season, flowing water may or not be present on the canyon floor.

Depression

A depression is an area surrounded by higher ground in all directions. On maps, a depression is represented by closed contour lines with tick marks pointing toward lower ground. Depressions include volcanic and impact craters. Lakes are water-filled depressions, but underwater contour lines are normally not shown on topographic maps.

1.9.5 How to interpret terrain on a map

The ability to interpret the terrain described on topographic maps is a critical skill needed for successful land navigation. Individually, terrain features can be difficult to distinguish because it is often tricky to tell whether adjacent contour lines signify an upward or downward slope. Everything on a map is interconnected, so the key to interpreting the terrain lies in your ability to figure out how your area of interest relates to the larger picture.

Try the following technique to figure out which portions of the map represent higher versus lower ground. Major lakes, rivers, and valleys are located on lower ground. Analyze the contour lines that cross the longest streams on the map to figure out which way the water is flowing. Any naturally flowing body of water runs downhill along the bottom of a valley, canyon, or gully. The bottom of these features is represented by V-shaped or U-shaped contour lines with the closed end of the contour lines pointing upstream. Determine the direction of the flow of all streams that feed into the major streams. On their upstream end, all streams eventually begin at a lake, gully, glacier, spring, or near a pass. Tracing out all the streams on the map will give you a picture of how the area is drained and where most of the lower ground is located.

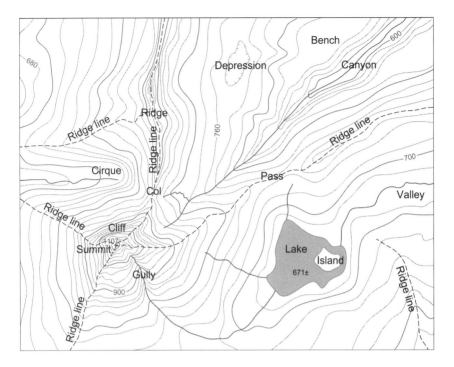

The higher ground is composed of ridges, summits, cols, and plateaus. On your map, connect the summits of mountains and hills with lines that follow the highest possible routes. These routes are mostly along ridgelines via passes, cols, and knolls. Then draw lines along ridges that radiate from the summits or fork off from the main ridges. Drawing these ridgelines will give you a sense of where the high ground is located.

Once you have identified the areas of high and low ground, it will be much easier for you to make out the terrain features in your area of interest.

1.10 Nautical charts

Nautical charts are essential for safe navigation on large bodies of water, especially along coastlines. Unlike maps, charts are specifically designed to describe water areas. The information included on a chart is even more wide-ranging than what you see on a map. Prevailing currents, shipping lanes, harbors, anchorages, reefs, sand bars, tidal flats, navigation aids, and much more are shown on a chart. It is important to thoroughly understand all the symbols. Consult the legend before leaving shore.

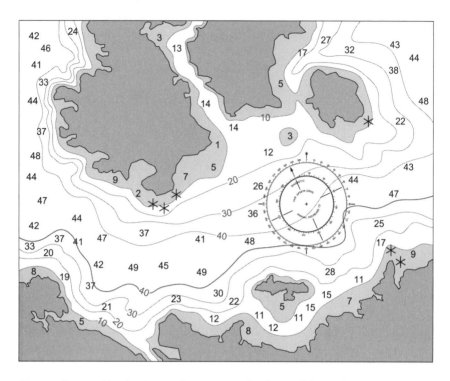

Contour lines and/or depth soundings portray the shape of the sea bottom. Instead of showing the elevation above sea level, the contour lines and soundings show the depth below sea level. Charts use the mean low water level, the average level of all the low tides at that location, as a vertical datum. A chart is not meant to just be viewed; it is used for plotting courses and lines of position. Like maps, charts are drawn to different scales and are made from various types of projections.

Chapter 2
Compass

Compasses have been around for many centuries, initially for ship navigation but later also for land navigation. A compass needle that is free to rotate will keep pointing in a specific direction. This enables a compass user to stay on course toward any desired direction, a powerful concept in navigation. Even today, the compass remains one of the most widely used navigation instruments.

2.1 Earth's magnetic field

2.1.1 Magnetic field theory

Deep inside Earth, the movement of molten metal generates a magnetic field that envelops Earth. This invisible force field permeates our surroundings. Its presence is felt inside Earth, on the surface, in the oceans, in the atmosphere, and in nearby space. The field varies in strength and direction depending on the location. It can be visualized as an array of lines with arrows pointing in the direction of the magnetic force. The strength of the magnetic force is proportional to how close the field lines are to each other.

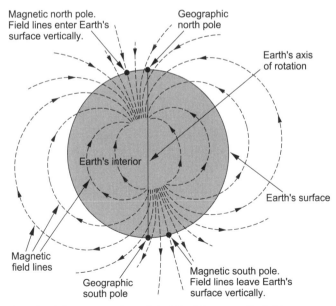

Idealized (bar magnet) model of Earth's magnetic field

Earth's magnetic field is shaped somewhat like the field of a bar magnet where the field lines leave the magnet at one end, curve around, and enter the magnet at the other end. The location where the magnetic field lines plunge vertically into Earth's surface is called the magnetic north pole. The location where the magnetic field lines leave Earth's surface vertically is called the magnetic south pole.

The real shape of Earth's magnetic field is a superposition of many magnetic fields corresponding to many molten metal flows inside Earth, as well as local magnetic anomalies caused by ore deposits. The resultant field is much more complicated than that of a single bar magnet. In fact, the magnetic poles are not on exact opposite sides of Earth, and the magnetic field lines generally don't follow the shortest path along Earth's surface to the nearest magnetic pole. The map below shows the approximate shape and direction of the magnetic field lines in polar regions.

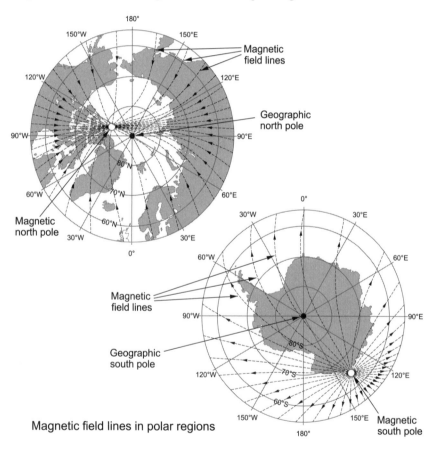

Magnetic field lines in polar regions

2.1.2 Magnetic pole movement

The shape of Earth's magnetic field is continually changing, causing the magnetic poles to move. Three types of magnetic pole movement have been observed: (1) secular movement where the magnetic poles move slowly over the years, (2) diurnal, or daily, movement around the average position, and (3) erratic movement where the magnetic poles jump rapidly from one position to another.

Secular movement

The molten metal flows inside Earth are continually changing, altering the shape of the magnetic field and shifting the average position of the magnetic poles in the process. The rate and direction of the magnetic pole movement is somewhat predictable. It typically ranges from a few kilometers to a few tens of kilometers per year. The secular movement must be taken into account when using a compass. The maps below show the secular movement over a 100-year period.

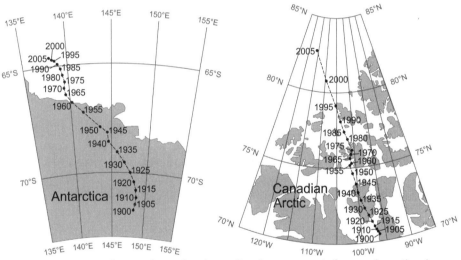

Secular movement of magnetic south pole   Secular movement of magnetic north pole

Diurnal movement

The sun continually emits electrically charged particles in all directions, creating something called the solar wind. When the solar wind reaches Earth, it pushes or pulls the magnetic poles to one side. As Earth rotates around its axis, the magnetic poles move around in an ellipse about their average positions. This is called the diurnal movement of the magnetic poles.

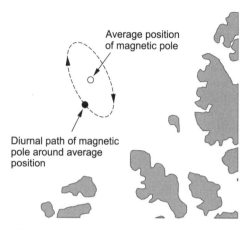

Diurnal movement of magnetic pole

Depending on the strength of the solar wind, the magnetic poles can be shifted by up to a few tens of kilometers about their average positions. The diurnal movement has negligible effect on the direction of a compass needle unless you happen to be close to one of the magnetic poles.

Erratic movement

The solar wind varies in intensity based on a cycle with an average period of 11 years that is closely tied to sunspot activity on the sun. The sun's magnetic activity reaches a maximum during each cycle and then usually quiets down for prolonged periods, although heightened activity can occur anytime. During periods of high magnetic activity, gusts of charged particles are hurled into space, distorting the magnetic field when reaching Earth. The magnetic poles can move about erratically, causing compass needles to swing wildly in the vicinity of the magnetic poles.

2.2 How a compass works

A compass needle is simply a strip of magnetized metal mounted on a swivel that lets the needle rotate freely. Any external magnetic field will generate a magnetic torque that attempts to align the needle along the external magnetic field lines. In the absence of other external fields, a freely rotating compass needle will align itself with Earth's local magnetic field line. The north-seeking end of the needle will point in the direction of the magnetic field line, but usually not directly toward the north magnetic pole.

Provided the compass needle is free to rotate, the magnetic torque will keep the needle pointed in the same direction regardless of how the base of the compass is oriented. By means of a mechanical linkage, this phenomenon can be used to keep the base of a compass pointed in any desired direction.

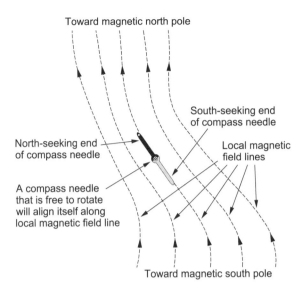

Toward magnetic north pole

South-seeking end
of compass needle

North-seeking end
of compass needle

Local magnetic
field lines

A compass needle
that is free to rotate
will align itself along
local magnetic field line

Toward magnetic south pole

Electronic compasses don't use magnetic needles but instead have sensitive magnetic sensors that determine the direction of the local magnetic field. The direction of the magnetic field is shown on a liquid crystal display as an arrow. Bearings can be stored in the internal memory of some electronic compasses.

A compass is primarily used to keep you pointed in a particular direction (bearing) as you travel, but can also be used to triangulate your position on a map. The accuracy of a standard compass is about two degrees in regions far away from the magnetic poles. At the magnetic poles, the compass needle would point straight up or down, making it useless for navigation. Other external magnetic fields, such as magnetism caused by power lines, local ore bodies, or lava flows can affect your compass needle or electronic compass.

Objects made from ferromagnetic materials will interfere with your compass if the object is close enough to the needle. The most common ferromagnetic materials contain iron or nickel. Before using your compass, test objects that you suspect are ferromagnetic or magnetized, such as belt buckles, ski poles, ice axes, tent poles, radios, or watches. Bring the object toward your compass and observe if, and at what distance, the needle moves. When navigating with a compass, make sure that all ferromagnetic or magnetized objects are kept far enough away to avoid interfering with your compass needle or digital compass.

2.3 Compass bearings

Depending on your navigation technique, compass bearings (directions) are measured relative to true (geographic) north, magnetic north, or grid north. The unit for measuring bearings is normally degrees, but gradians or other units are used on some compasses. There are 360 degrees (°), or 400 gradians (grad or gr), in one full rotation. Military compasses use the unit milliradian (mil) to measure bearings. There are 6283.1853... mils in one full circle, although most military compasses round off this number to 6000, 6400, or some other intermediate number.

True bearings

True compass bearings are measured as angles relative to the direction of the geographic north pole. They are always measured clockwise from the direction to the north pole, even in the southern hemisphere.

Each of the familiar cardinal directions is equivalent to a particular true bearing: north (0°), east (90°), south (180°), and west (270°). Midway in between are the intermediate directions: northeast (45°), southeast (135°), southwest (225°), and northwest (315°). These directions can be further subdivided into north-northeast (22.5°), east-northeast (67.5°), east-southeast (112.5°), south-southeast (157.5°), south-southwest (202.5°), west-southwest (247.5°), west-northwest (292.5°), and north-northwest (337.5°).

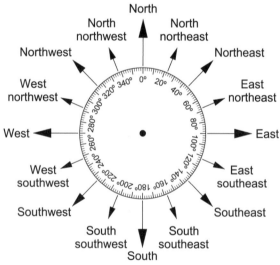

Cardinal and intermediate directions

Example of true compass bearings

Below are several direction arrows on a chart. Each arrow represents a particular true bearing.

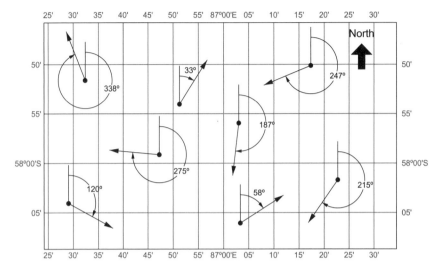

Note that although this chart represents a portion of the southern hemisphere, the bearings are relative to the geographic north pole, not the south pole. Longitudes are by definition north-south lines and are therefore convenient reference lines from which true bearings can be measured.

Magnetic and grid bearings

In certain navigation applications, compass bearings are measured relative to magnetic north or grid north instead of true north. Magnetic north is defined as the direction of the magnetic field at your location. Grid north is the direction of the north-pointing end of your map's north-south grid lines.

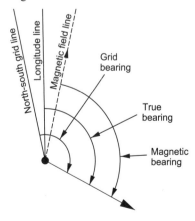

2.4 Magnetic declination

Magnetic field lines are not aligned north-south across most of Earth's surface. This means that the north seeking end of a compass needle will, in most cases, point in a direction other than toward the geographic north pole. When navigating with a map and compass, you must consider this effect whenever it causes a bearing error of more than a couple of degrees.

2.4.1 Magnetic declination theory

Most people mistakenly believe that a freely rotating compass needle points directly toward the nearest magnetic pole. This would only be true if magnetic field lines followed the shortest path along Earth's surface from your compass to the nearest magnetic pole, which is generally not the case.

The magnetic declination (variation) at a specific location is the angle between the direction of the north-seeking end of the needle and the direction to the geographic north pole. This definition applies everywhere on Earth including in the southern hemisphere. Since longitudes are perfect north-south lines along Earth's surface, the magnetic declination at your location can be defined as the angle between the north-seeking end of your compass needle and the north-pointing portion of your local longitude. If the north-seeking end of the needle points west (left) of the longitude, the declination is west, and if the needle points east (right) of the longitude, the declination is east.

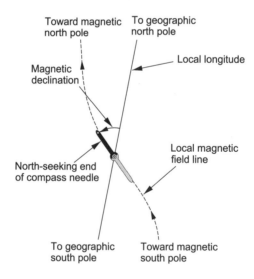

To state the magnetic declination, write the angle followed by the label "E" or "W" to indicate whether it's east or west, for example 93°E. By definition the declination is always somewhere between 180°W and 180°E.

Examples of magnetic declination:

The maps below show eight freely rotating compass needles at random locations in the southern and northern hemispheres. The table shows how the magnetic declination is derived for each location.

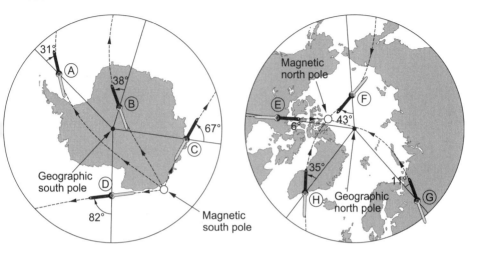

Location	Angle relative to longitude	Direction relative to geographic north pole	Magnetic declination
A	31°	right (east)	31°E
B	38°	left (west)	38°W
C	67°	left (west)	67°W
D	82°	right (east)	82°E
E	6°	left (west)	6°W
F	43°	right (east)	43°E
G	11°	right (east)	11°E
H	35°	left (west)	35°W

2.4.2 Estimating magnetic declination

The secular movement of Earth's magnetic field causes the declination to change over the years. Five different ways to estimate the magnetic declination at your location are described here: (1) declination diagram, (2) compass rose, (3) computer software, (4) GPS receiver, and (5) direct measurement.

Declination diagram

Most high-quality topographic maps have a diagram that shows the magnetic declination for the area covered by the map. Usually, the date and the annual rate of change when the declination was measured are also shown. The older the declination date, the more inaccurate the stated declination and annual change are likely to be. On some maps, the declination and date are written without an associated diagram.

Figuring out how to calculate the declination from a diagram may require some work, made even more challenging if you're unfamiliar with the language used on the map. Some diagrams give you the declination relative to both geographic (true) and grid north. For land navigation, use grid north if you have a choice because you will likely be taking bearings relative to the map's grid.

Examples of declination from diagrams:

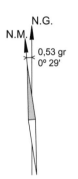

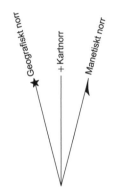

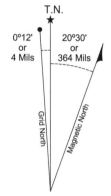

La déclinaison magnétique correspond au centre de la feuille au 1er janvier 1998 Elle diminue chaque année de 0,12 gr (0° 6')

Meridiankonvergensen (skillnaden mellan kartnorr och geografisk norr) är i kartbladeds centrum +2,3°. Kompassens missgivning (skillnaden mellan magnetiskt och geografiskt norr) 2000 - 2005 är 5.0° ostlig.

Use diagram only to obtain numerical values. Approximate mean declination 1996 for centre of map. Annual change decreasing 8.0'

The left diagram is taken from a French map. It gives the declination as 0,53 gr or 0°29'. The date is given as 1998 with an annual decrease of 0,12 gr or 0°6'. Ignore the "gr" unit unless your compass dial is marked in gradians. N.G. stands for geographic north, and N.M. stands for magnetic north. In 1998 the compass needle would have pointed 29' left (west) of true north, giving a declination of 0°29'W. If the year is now 2005, the declination has decreased by 7 x 6' = 42' giving you a declination of 29'W - 42' = -13'W or 0°13'E. Rounding off this number to the nearest degree gives you a declination of 0°. In other words, ignore the declination when navigating with this map.

The middle diagram is taken from a Swedish map. The arrow on the right stands for magnetic north and the line with the star stands for geographic north. The middle line with "+" on top stands for map (grid) north. Magnetic north is given as +2,3° right (east) of grid north and 5,0° east of geographic north. Neither the year when the declination was measured, nor the annual rate of change is given. According to the map, the declination is valid only for a range of years (2000 - 2005). If the year is now 2008, you will have no choice but to use the given declination. You do however have a choice between grid north and geographic north. Choose grid north (2.3°E) and round off this declination to 2°E.

The right diagram shows a magnetic arrow pointing 20º30' (364 mils) to the right or east of geographic (true) north (T.N.). An added angle of 0º12' (4 mils) is given between geographic north and grid north. The declination year is 1996 with an annual decrease of 8.0'. Ignore the "mil" unit unless you're using a military compass. Choosing grid north and assuming the year is now 2006 gives you a declination of 20º30'E + 0º12' - 10 x 8.0' = 20º30' + 12' - 80' = 20º30'E - 68' = 20º30'E - 1º08' = 19º22'E. Round off this number to 19ºE.

Compass Rose

Nautical charts use one or more compass roses instead of a declination diagram. A compass rose consists of an inner graduated ring that shows magnetic bearings, nested inside an outer graduated ring that shows true bearings. In marine terminology, declination is called "variation." On a compass rose, the variation is the difference between any bearing on the inner ring, versus the same bearing on the outer ring. In addition, the variation as well as the date and annual rate of change are usually written inside the inner ring.

Example of variation from compass rose

The compass rose below shows a variation of 24º38'W for 2004, with an annual decrease of 7.2'. If the year is now 2012, the variation would be 24º38'W - 8 x 7.2' = 24º38' - 57.6' = 23º40.4'W. Round off this number to 24ºW.

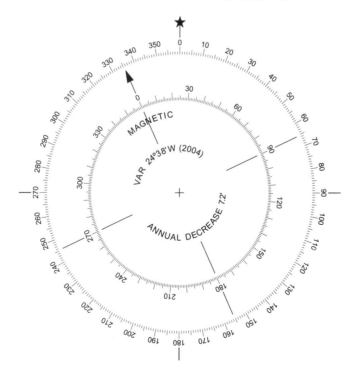

Computer software

Computer programs are available that calculate the magnetic declination for any point on Earth's surface. Just type in your position coordinates, the date, and the year. The program displays the declination. Be aware that the calculations are based on the shape of Earth's magnetic field and predicted future values at the time that the software was developed. Since magnetic field changes are somewhat unpredictable, use the latest version of the software for best accuracy. Find out whether the declination is given relative to geographic north or grid north. Some programs let you choose between the two systems.

GPS receiver

GPS receivers are equipped with software that estimates and displays the magnetic declination. Look in your GPS user manual for a way to display the magnetic declination at your location. Most receivers give you the declination relative to both geographic and grid north. GPS receivers use declination data based on the annual rate of change when the GPS software was developed. The receiver will therefore suffer from inaccurate declinations as it ages. Download new software with updated declination data into your receiver whenever the software becomes available. Future enhancements may allow declination data to be beamed directly from the GPS satellites to your receiver.

Direct declination measurement

With a map and compass, you can directly measure the magnetic declination if you know your location on the map and can identify a nearby landmark. Direct measurement is the surest way to determine your declination. It takes into account all the local and global anomalies.

1. Pinpoint your position on the map as accurately as possible. Use a GPS receiver if you have one.
2. Take a bearing off your map (Section 2.6.1) from your present location to an identifiable landmark and note the resultant bearing. For example 271°.
3. Take a field bearing off the same landmark (Section 2.6.2) and note the resultant bearing. For example 302°.
4. Your declination number is the difference between the map bearing and the field bearing: 302° - 271° = 31°.
5. Look at the graduated dial of your compass. If the field bearing is clockwise from your map bearing, the declination is west. If it is counterclockwise, the declination is east. In this example, the field bearing (302°) is clockwise from the map bearing (271°) so your declination is 31°W.

Be careful with bearings on either side of the 0° mark. Let's say you take bearings off a second landmark, and get a map bearing of 334° and a field bearing of 7°. This gives you a declination number of 334° - 7° = 327°, but by definition, the declination number cannot be more than 180°. To correct this, subtract your initial declination number from 360°. This yields a declination of 360° - 327° = 33°W. Averaging this results with the first measurement (31°W) gives a declination of 32°W. For even more confidence in your results, repeat the process with additional landmarks.

2.4.3 Compensating for magnetic declination

You must compensate for the magnetic declination whenever you use a compass together with a map. This applies to both mechanical and electronic compasses. There are two ways to compensate for the magnetic declination: (1) using a compass with an adjustable declination mechanism, or (2) adding or subtracting the declination after taking a compass bearing. You could also do all your navigation relative to magnetic north, which is often done in marine navigation.

Compass with adjustable declination mechanism

For land navigation, the author recommends that you use a compass with an adjustable declination mechanism. Just set the declination to the correct value, and then forget about declination until you move into an area with a different declination.

Many types of adjustable mechanisms exist. Look in your compass manual for instructions on how to adjust the declination. Be aware that salt water or dirt can seize the mechanism, thereby turning your adjustable compass into a nonadjustable type. Most electronic compasses have built-in functions to adjust the declination.

Example of declination mechanism

A widely-used declination mechanism for an orienteering compass consists of a small screw located on the backside of the housing. Use a small screwdriver to turn the screw until the scale shows the correct declination for your location. Note that the orienting arrow moves relative to the meridian lines when you turn the screw.

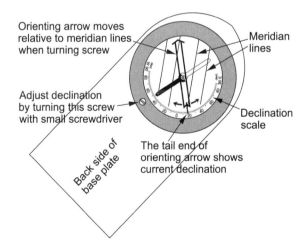

Compass without declination mechanism

On a compass without an adjustable declination mechanism, you must add or subtract the appropriate declination after taking a bearing. Whether you add or subtract depends on whether the declination is east or west and whether you're going from a map to the real world or vice versa (Table 2.4). Adding means turning the graduated dial counterclockwise, while subtracting means turning it clockwise. Pay attention to what you're doing. It's easy to do mistakes, especially if you have to turn the dial past the zero mark.

Table 2.4 - Declination adjustments		
Declination	**Map to real world**	**Real world to map**
east	subtract	add
west	add	subtract

Compensating for declination - Example 1

Let's say the declination is 31°W. You've taken a bearing of 352° off a map (Section 2.6.1), and want to follow this bearing in the real world (Section 2.6.3). Table 2.4 tells you to add the declination because you're going from a map to the real world. The adjusted bearing becomes 352° + 31° = 383°. By definition, bearings must be between 0° and 360°, so subtract 360°. Set you compass to 383° - 360° = 23° before following this bearing.

Compensating for declination - Example 2

The declination is 18°E. You've taken a field bearing of 126° off a landmark (Section 2.6.2) and want to triangulate your position on the map. In this case, you're going from the real world to a map. Table 2.4 tells you to add the declination. Set your compass to 126° + 18° = 144° before placing the compass on the map.

2.5 Magnetic dip

Magnetic dip, also known as inclination, is the angle between level ground and the magnetic field line at your location. The dip is by definition 90° (vertical) at the magnetic poles and is 0° (horizontal) in some regions between the poles. In most parts of the world, the dip is somewhere between these two extremes. Because the compass needle tries to align itself along the local magnetic field line, the dip causes the needle to point upward or downward. If the dip is too large, the needle will rub against the top or bottom of the housing, preventing the needle from rotating freely.

Most high-quality compasses try to compensate for magnetic dip by using a counterweight on one end of the needle. Because the magnetic dip varies across Earth's surface, a compass with a counterweight designed for a certain area will not work elsewhere. Before purchasing a compass, make sure it is designed for the area that you intend to travel.

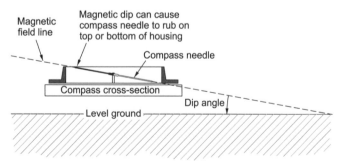

Some compasses feature deep well designs with lots of pivot room for the compass needle. Other designs use a multi-pivot mechanism to keep the needle level. These so-called world compasses can be used anywhere in the world except at extreme dip locations such as near the magnetic poles.

You may be able to compensate for the magnetic dip by holding your compass at an angle. This makes the operation of the compass more difficult, particularly with a mirror compass. Electronic compasses will function anywhere but become less accurate with increasing dip. Most marine compasses are balanced for the dip of a particular area, although they usually work in other areas but become less accurate.

2.6 Orienteering compass

For land navigation, you need a compass with a base plate. Without a base plate, you cannot use your compass to take bearings off a map. Both mirror and standard orienteering compasses are fitted with a base plate, and either type is good for wilderness navigation. A mirror compass is more accurate for aiming at a target, but is more difficult to use than a standard orienteering compass. Most procedures in this book assume that you are using a standard compass, but this should not be a concern for someone using a mirror compass. Except for the aiming process, both types of compasses are used in exactly the same manner. Some orienteering compasses have a built-in inclinometer that lets you measure the steepness of slopes. If you're familiar with trigonometry, you can use the inclinometer to measure heights of features.

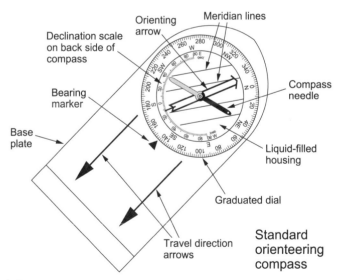

Standard orienteering compass

Base plate

The base plate, made of transparent plastic, is more than a structural component. Its long edges are used for taking bearings off a map or for drawing triangulation lines on the map. The travel direction arrow(s) and bearing marker are imprinted on the base plate. Most base plates are inscribed with scales of various units that can be used as rulers.

Compass needle

The compass needle is a magnetized strip of metal that is balanced on a pivot joint. The north-seeking end of the needle is usually painted red and the south seeking end white or black, but some compasses use other color combinations.

Travel-direction arrows

One or more travel-direction arrows are imprinted on the base plate and show the travel direction when following a compass bearing. They are also used for taking a field bearing. On a mirror compass, a sighting notch or a mirror line is used instead of travel-direction arrows.

Housing with graduated dial

The housing is a liquid-filled container that encloses the compass needle. The liquid is used to dampen the movement of the needle. The perimeter of the housing consists of a graduated dial that is marked with bearings from 0° through 360°. Some compasses use other angle units. To adjust the compass bearing, rotate the housing and read off the bearing on the bearing marker located on the base plate.

Meridian lines

The meridian lines make it easier to align the housing north-south on the map when taking bearings or drawing lines of position. The meridian lines are mechanically linked with the housing and move together as one unit.

Orienting arrow

The orienting arrow is used to correctly align the base plate relative to the compass needle when following a compass bearing or taking a field bearing.

Declination mechanism

Some compasses have a built-in declination mechanism. The declination mechanism compensates for the error between magnetic and geographic bearings by adjusting the angle of the orienting arrow relative to the graduated dial. The declination is adjusted manually and read off the declination scale.

2.6.1 Taking a bearing off a map

Taking a bearing off a map is an elementary concept in compass navigation. It involves using a map and orienteering compass to measure the direction toward a selected target.

1. Use terrain association (Section 8.1), a GPS receiver, or any other method to determine your location on the map.

2. If your compass is equipped with an adjustable magnetic declination mechanism, adjust the declination so that it conforms to grid north.

3. Place your compass on the map. The map can be oriented in any direction. Align the base plate with an imaginary straight line that passes through both your present location and your desired target. Make sure the travel-direction arrows on the base plate (or mirror line) point toward your desired target on the map, not the reverse direction.

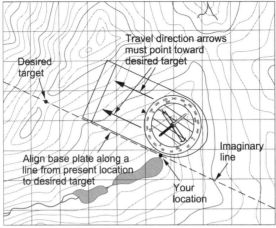

Step 3: Place and align compass on map

4. Without moving the base plate, turn the graduated dial until the meridian lines on the compass are parallel to the north-south grid lines on the map. Make sure north (0°) on the graduated dial points toward north on the map and not south.

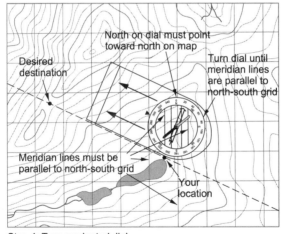

Step 4: Turn graduated dial

5. Remove your compass from the map and read off the bearing. You may want to record this bearing for later use.

6. If your compass lacks an adjustable declination mechanism, adjust the graduated dial by the appropriate declination number. Since you're going from a map to the real world, subtract the declination number for an east declination, add for a west declination.

2.6.2 Taking a field bearing

Taking a field bearing involves measuring the direction to a terrain feature in the real world. Three primary reasons exist for taking a field bearing: (1) determining your position by triangulation, (2) staying on track toward an intermittently visible target, or (3) directly measuring the magnetic declination.

1. If your compass is equipped with an adjustable magnetic declination mechanism, adjust the declination so that it conforms to grid north. Actually, this only applies if the bearing is going to be used for triangulation. If the bearing is used to stay on track toward the landmark or to measure the declination, the declination setting is arbitrary as long at it is kept constant throughout the procedure.

2. Aim the travel direction arrows (or mirror line) of the compass toward the landmark whose direction you want to measure.

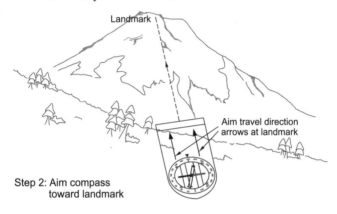

Landmark

Aim travel direction arrows at landmark

Step 2: Aim compass toward landmark

3. While keeping the base plate level and the travel-direction arrows pointed toward the landmark, turn the graduated dial until the north-seeking end of the compass needle lines up with the north end of the orienting arrow. Read off the bearing.

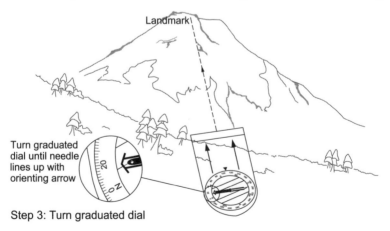

Landmark

Turn graduated dial until needle lines up with orienting arrow

Step 3: Turn graduated dial

4. If your compass lacks an adjustable declination mechanism, adjust the graduated dial by the appropriate declination number before performing a triangulation. Since you're going from the real world to a map, add the declination number for an east declination, subtract for a west declination. Don't adjust anything if the bearing is for keeping track of your direction toward the landmark. The compass is obviously already pointing in the correct direction. The same applies for a bearing taken to measure the declination. You cannot compensate for an unknown declination that you are about to calculate.

2.6.3 Following a compass bearing

Following a compass bearing is what you do in the real world after taking either a map or a field bearing. As you travel, the compass shows you the direction to your chosen target.

1. Hold the compass in front of you with the travel direction arrows (or mirror line) pointing directly ahead.

2. While keeping the base plate level, turn your body together with the compass until the north-seeking end of the compass needle coincides with the north end of the orienting arrow. The travel-direction arrows or mirror line will now point toward your target.

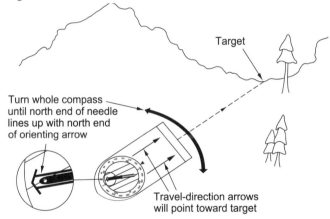

Target

Turn whole compass until north end of needle lines up with north end of orienting arrow

Travel-direction arrows will point toward target

3. Follow the travel direction arrows or the mirror line toward the target.

To avoid constantly looking at your compass, follow a series steering marks along your line of travel. A steering mark can be any recognizable feature in line with your compass bearing. If you have a choice, select the highest and most distant feature. Keep in mind that a feature can change appearance as you move toward it. If a steering mark is beyond your target, be careful not to overshoot your target. During poor visibility, you may have to select steering marks that are very close together. This will necessitate frequent checks of your compass, and in extreme cases such as whiteouts, you may be forced to continuously look at your compass.

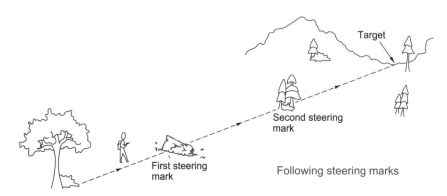

Following steering marks

If you cannot follow the compass bearing because of an intervening obstacle, go around the obstacle and then try to regain your original line of travel. This is easy if there is a steering mark on the far side of the obstacle. After circumventing the obstacle, just go to the steering mark to regain your original line of travel.

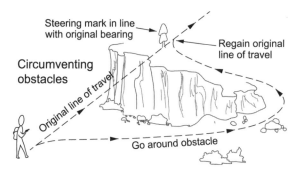

If there is no steering mark on the far side of the obstacle, use a back bearing (described next) or dead reckoning (Section 8.3.3) to regain your line of travel.

Using a back bearing

A back bearing is the opposite direction from your original bearing to the target. Pointing your compass along a back bearing will reveal if you are drifting off course and help you regain your line of travel after circumventing an obstacle.

1. Leave all the compass settings unchanged from your original bearing.

2. Turn your body together with the compass until the south-seeking end of the compass needle coincides with the north end of the orienting arrow. This effectively reverses your original bearing and the travel direction arrows will point in the opposite direction from your target.

3. If you're on track, the back bearing will point directly toward a steering mark along your previously traveled route. If it doesn't, move sideways until the back bearing points directly toward the steering mark. You will then have regained your original line of travel.

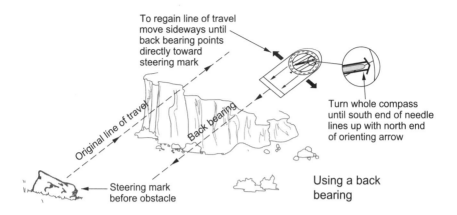

To regain line of travel move sideways until back bearing points directly toward steering mark

Turn whole compass until south end of needle lines up with north end of orienting arrow

Original line of travel

Back bearing

Steering mark before obstacle

Using a back bearing

2.6.4 Triangulating from a linear feature

With a map and compass, all you need is one visible landmark to pinpoint your position, provided you're located on, or near, a linear feature such as a trail, road, power line, narrow ridge, river, or lake shore.

1. If your compass is equipped with an adjustable magnetic declination mechanism, adjust the declination so that it conforms to grid north.

2. Aim your compass toward an identifiable landmark and take a field bearing off that landmark (Section 2.6.2). For best accuracy, pick the nearest landmark that is approximately perpendicular to the linear feature.

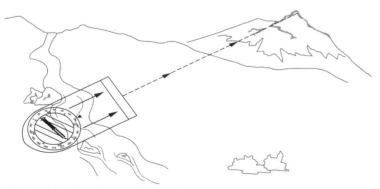

Step 2: Take a bearing off a landmark

3. If your compass lacks an adjustable declination mechanism, adjust the graduated dial by the appropriate declination number. Since you're going from the real world to a map, add the declination number for an east declination, subtract for a west declination.

4. Place the compass on the map with a corner of the base plate on the landmark.

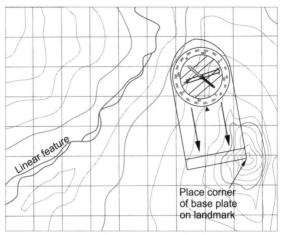

Step 4: Place corner of compass on landmark

5. Using the corner of the base plate as a pivot point, rotate the whole compass until the meridian lines on the compass are parallel to the north-south grid lines on the map. Make sure north (0°) on the graduated dial points toward north on the map, not south. Do not rotate the graduated dial during this step.
6. On the map, draw a straight line (real or imaginary) parallel to the base plate from the landmark to the linear feature that you are on. Your position is where the straight line and the linear feature intersect.

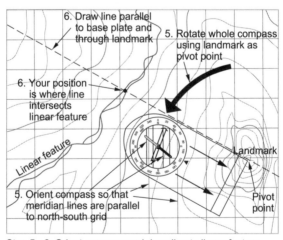

Step 5 - 6: Orient compass and draw line to linear feature

If you intend to return to this position, record the field bearing that you have taken off the landmark (Step 2). On your return, first find your way back to the linear feature. Set the compass to the recorded bearing and then aim the compass like you would if you were following the bearing. If the compass points to the right of the landmark, move left along the linear feature to reach the recorded position; if the compass points to the left of the landmark, move to the right. When the compass points directly at the landmark, you will have reached your recorded position.

2.6.5 Triangulating off multiple landmarks

With a map and compass, you can pinpoint your location anywhere on the map by taking field bearings off two or more landmarks.

1. Use your compass to take a field bearing off a landmark. For best accuracy, select the nearest identifiable landmark.

2. Place the compass on the map with a corner of the base plate on the landmark.

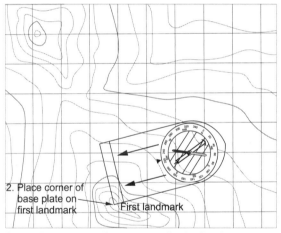

Step 2: Place corner of compass on first landmark

3. Using the corner of the base plate as a pivot point, rotate the whole compass until the meridian lines on the compass are parallel to the north-south grid lines on the map. Make sure north (0°) on the graduated dial points toward north on the map, not south. Do not rotate the graduated dial during this step.

4. On the map, draw a straight line (real or imaginary) parallel to the base plate and through the landmark. This is your first line of position.

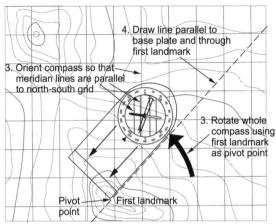

Step 3 - 4: Orient compass and draw line

5. Use your compass to take a field bearing off a second landmark. For best accuracy, the direction to the second landmark should be approximately perpendicular to the first landmark.

6. Place the compass on the map with a corner of the base plate on the second landmark.

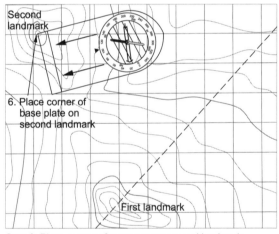

Step 6: Place corner of compass on second landmark

7. Using the corner of the base plate as a pivot point, rotate the base plate until the meridian lines on the compass are parallel to the north-south grid lines on the map.

8. Draw a straight line parallel to the base plate and through the second landmark. This is your second line of position. Your location is the intersection between the first and second line of position.

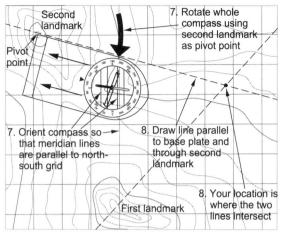

Step 7 - 8: Orient compass and draw second line

9. To confirm that you've done the triangulation correctly, repeat the process with bearings off additional landmarks. If you've done your triangulation correctly, all lines of position will intersect.

2.7 Marine compass

A marine compass is designed to work on a pitching boat. Most types of marine compasses are permanently attached to the boat, but there are also handheld units equipped with a sight for taking field bearings. The techniques for taking and following bearings with a marine compass are different than with an orienteering compass.

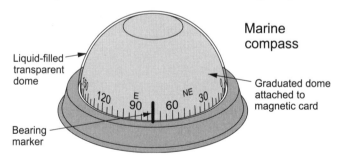

Instead of a needle, a marine compass uses a magnetic card. The card is mounted on a base assembly via gimbals that keep the card level as the boat rocks. The bearing numbers are either marked directly on the magnetic card or on a graduated dome attached to the card. The card assembly is enclosed inside a liquid-filled, transparent dome. A line inscribed on the transparent dome serves as a bearing marker.

Marine compasses generally do not have a declination mechanism, but some are equipped with adjustable magnets that are designed to compensate for interfering ferromagnetic material on the vessel.

2.7.1 Taking a bearing off a nautical chart

A standard marine compass cannot be used to take a bearing off a chart or map because the compass lacks a base plate and is part of the boat. Most ocean navigators use a plotting tool instead. Many types of plotting tools are available, including protractors, parallel rulers, and specially designed course plotters. Some plotting tools are used in conjunction with the chart's compass rose. You could also use an orienteering compass to take the bearing (Section 2.6.1). Before purchasing a plotting tool, make sure it is suitable for use on your watercraft. To take accurate bearings, you need a conveniently located flat surface that is reasonably protected from the elements.

The following procedure describes how to use a set of parallel rulers to take a bearing off a nautical chart. The chart must have at least one compass rose.

1. Place the parallel rulers on the chart. The chart can be oriented in any direction. Align one edge of the ruler with an imaginary straight line that passes through both your present location and your desired target.

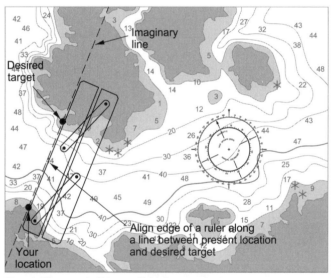

Step 1: Place and align parallel rulers on chart

2. Walk the rulers over to the nearest compass rose by alternately holding down one ruler while moving the other ruler. Be careful not to lose the initial orientation of the rulers during the walk. Align one edge of the ruler with the center point of the compass rose.
3. Read the magnetic or true bearing off the compass rose. In most marine applications, the navigation is done with magnetic bearings. The reverse bearing can be read off on the opposite side of the compass rose.

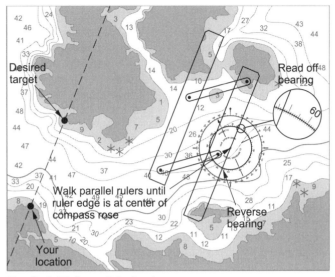

Step 2 - 3: Walk parallel rulers to compass rose
and read off bearing

2.7.2 Taking a field bearing with a marine compass

To take a field bearing with a marine compass, use the hull of your boat as a base plate and the bow as a travel direction arrow.

1. Position yourself along the centerline of the boat. Turn the boat until the bow points directly toward your selected landmark.

2. Read the bearing off your boat's compass and record the bearing. Most marine compasses show magnetic bearings.

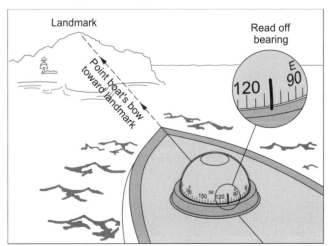

Step 1 - 2: Point bow toward landmark and read off bearing

2.7.3 Following a compass bearing on the water

Following a compass bearing on the water is more complicated than on land. On land, your primary hurdle is circumventing obstacles without losing you course. On the water, you are faced with the considerable challenge of adjusting your heading to compensate for the drift caused by currents, winds, and waves.

1. Estimate the anticipated forward speed of your vessel relative to the water in the direction of your target. Let's say for example that your target is at a magnetic bearing of 180°, and you expect your average speed to be 3.5 knots (nautical miles per hour) in that direction.

2. Find the average speed and direction of the water current between you and your target. Your chart may provide this information. In areas subjected to tidal currents, you need a clock and tidal current tables that show the current at specific dates and times. Suppose for example that the average current between you and your target will be 1 knot at a magnetic bearing of 230° during your journey.

3. Recalculate your bearing and speed to compensate for the current. This is easiest done graphically on your chart with the help of plotting tools. Choose any convenient and consistent distance unit to represent speed. For example, let 1 cm represent 1 knot. Draw a line 3.5 cm long in the magnetic direction of 180° to represent your boat's 3.5-knot forward speed. At the end of this line, draw another line 1 cm long in the direction of 230° to represent the 1-knot current. Draw a line from the start of the first line to the end of the second line. The third line represents your recalculated bearing and speed. Measuring the direction and length of this line gives a bearing of 165° and a length of 3 cm. These numbers represent the boat's anticipated magnetic bearing (165°) and speed (3 knots) relative to solid ground.

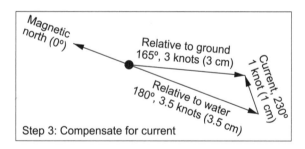

Step 3: Compensate for current

4. Determine the drift caused by wind and waves. This type of drift is difficult to calculate ahead of time because it changes as your heading changes. The surest way to correct for the drift is to do it after your boat is underway. The key factor to remember is that your boat is moving in the direction of the wake, not where the bow is pointing. Point the bow of your boat toward your anticipated bearing (165°). Estimate the direction of the boat's wake by looking back at the wake from the center of your compass. In this case, the wake is in line with 175°.

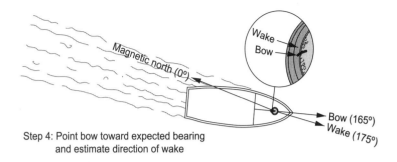

Step 4: Point bow toward expected bearing
and estimate direction of wake

5. To compensate for the drift caused by wind and waves, turn the boat until the wake lines up with your anticipated bearing (165°). Read the boat's new heading off the bearing marker (150°), and follow this heading to your target.

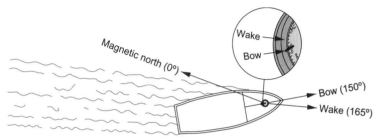

Step 5: Orient the boat until wake is in line with expected bearing

You may have to go through several iterations of this procedure because compensating for wind and waves changes your speed relative to the water, which in turn changes your numbers in Step 1 - 3.

2.8 Orienting a map or chart

A map or chart is oriented when geographic north on the map or chart corresponds to geographic north in the real world. It is much easier to compare what you see on the map with the real world when the map is oriented. Several techniques will accomplish this. The most reliable methods require a compass. Depending on your direction of travel, an oriented map or chart could be upside down, sideways, or at some other abnormal angle, making the text on the map difficult to read.

2.8.1 By terrain association

Orienting a map by terrain association means turning the map until what you see in the real world lines up with what you see on the map. Imagine yourself reduced in size by the same ratio as the map scale, and then placed on the map at your present location. In which direction and how far away would the surrounding landmarks be? Imagine a giant turning the map until the landmarks on the map point in the same direction as the corresponding real world landmarks. The map would then be oriented.

After turning the map, make sure that each visible linear feature in the real world is parallel to the same linear feature on the map, and don't ignore the alignment of features behind you. Also, check that the orientation isn't off by 180°. Terrain association is the quickest and easiest way to orient a map or chart, but lacks the precision of using a compass.

2.8.2 With orienteering compass and grid lines

Using a compass and the map's grid lines to orient the map is a very accurate method, provided your magnetic declination adjustment is correct.

1. If your compass is equipped with an adjustable magnetic declination mechanism, adjust the declination so that it conforms to grid north and then turn the graduated dial to north (0°). If your compass lacks an adjustable declination mechanism, turn the graduated dial to 0° and then adjust the dial by the appropriate declination number. Since you're going from a map to the real world, subtract the declination number for an east declination, add for a west declination.

2. Place your compass on the map. Align the base plate along one of the north-south grid lines and with the travel direction arrows pointing toward north on the map.

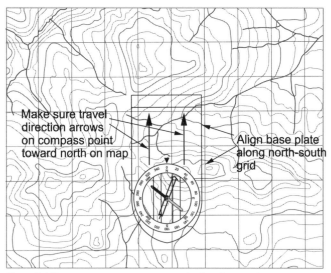

Step 2: Place compass on map and align base plate

3. Turn the map together with the compass until the north-seeking end of the compass needle coincides with the north end of the orienting arrow. Keep the compass level during this operation to ensure that the compass needle can rotate freely. The map is now oriented.

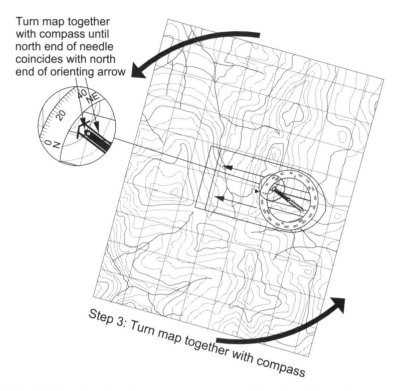

Turn map together with compass until north end of needle coincides with north end of orienting arrow

Step 3: Turn map together with compass

2.8.3 With orienteering compass and declination diagram

This method can only be used if there is a declination diagram on your map. It is generally less accurate than using the map's grid lines because it does not compensate for the declination change since the map was created. Another potentially serious error can occur if the declination diagram isn't drawn to angular scale.

1. Place your compass on the map with the center of the needle near the origin of the declination diagram. The orientation of the compass or the adjustment on the declination mechanism doesn't matter.

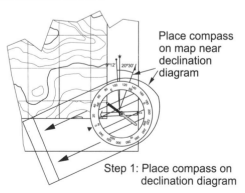

Place compass on map near declination diagram

Step 1: Place compass on declination diagram

2. Turn the map together with the compass until magnetic north on the declination diagram points in the same direction as the north-seeking end of the compass needle. Make sure the compass needle is free to rotate during this operation. The map is now approximately oriented.

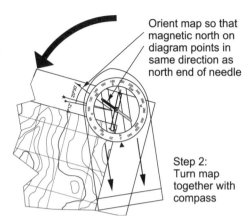

Orient map so that magnetic north on diagram points in same direction as north end of needle

Step 2: Turn map together with compass

2.8.4 With marine compass and compass rose

You cannot place a marine compass on a chart because the compass is usually attached to the boat. This makes it more difficult to orient a chart with a marine compass than with an orienteering compass. You are forced to place the chart beside the compass, which is a less accurate process.

1. Bring the chart as close as possible to the marine compass. Line up the center of a compass rose with both the center of the compass and the bearing marker.

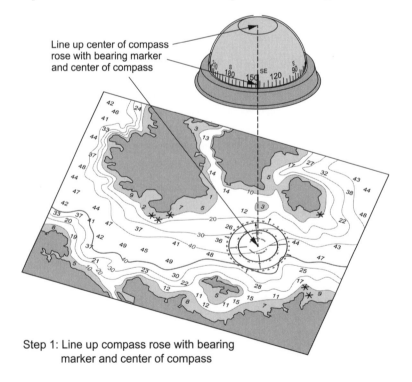

Line up center of compass rose with bearing marker and center of compass

Step 1: Line up compass rose with bearing marker and center of compass

2. Read the bearing off the bearing marker; for example 143° magnetic. Using the center of the compass rose as a pivot point, turn the chart until 143° on the magnetic ring of the compass rose points toward 143° on the compass dial. Make sure the center of the rose, the bearing marker, and the center of the compass are still lined up. The chart is now oriented.

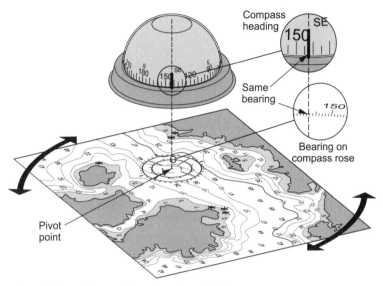

Compass heading

Same bearing

Bearing on compass rose

Pivot point

Step 2: Turn chart until compass heading lines up
with same bearing on compass rose

Alternatively, you could orient your chart so that magnetic north on the chart points toward the bow of your boat, and then turn the boat until the bow points toward magnetic north.

Chapter 3
Altimeter

3.1 How altimeters work

The air pressure in Earth's atmosphere is proportional to the weight of the overlying air. The higher your go, the less air remains above you, and therefore the lower the air pressure. In mathematical terms, the air pressure decreases logarithmically with increasing elevation. This relationship is called the pressure gradient of the atmosphere. An altimeter measures the ambient air pressure, and then calculates its elevation based on a predetermined pressure gradient. Two basic types of altimeters exist, mechanical and electronic.

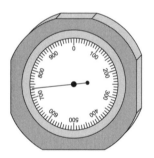
Mechanical altimeter

Digital altimeter

Wristwatch altimeter

A mechanical altimeter consists of a sealed chamber with a flexible wall that is mechanically linked to a rotating needle. The pressure inside the chamber stays more or less constant while the outside air pressure varies according to your altitude and other factors. The ambient air pressure expands or contracts the chamber wall, causing the mechanically linked needle to rotate by an amount proportional to the ambient air pressure. The needle rotates in front of a graduated dial that displays the elevation.

On electronic altimeters, the ambient air pressure expands or contracts a diaphragm that covers a sealed chamber. A built-in piezoresistive sensor deforms together with the diaphragm. The electrical resistance of the piezoresistive sensor changes in proportion to how much it expands or contracts. An electronic circuit measures the resistance across the sensor, and then converts the result into an elevation reading that is shown as a number on a liquid crystal display. Many other types of pressure sensing methods exist for electronic altimeters.

Altimeters are designed to work up to a maximum altitude. Taking the altimeter higher than the maximum allowable altitude may damage the unit. Keep this in mind when traveling in an airliner. Carry your altimeter with you in the pressurized cabin, not in the unpressurized baggage compartment. Generally, altimeters with lower maximum allowable altitudes are more accurate. Electronic altimeters tend to be lighter than mechanical altimeters and usually have the ability to store elevation readings. They are however more prone to failure, especially in cold weather when the batteries can go dead. Mechanical altimeters are rugged and dependable, and do not require batteries.

If you stay at one elevation, altimeters are able to measure or track ambient pressure changes. This can be useful for weather forecasting. For example, a rapid decrease in air pressure may be a precursor to an approaching storm.

Altimeters are easy to use. Just look at the display to see your elevation. Before reading the elevation of a mechanical altimeter, tap the front of the unit a couple of times to make sure the needle is not stuck in one position. Some electronic altimeters update their readings at periodic time intervals. During a rapid ascent or descent, you may have to stop and wait a few moments for the display to show the updated elevation.

3.2 Calibrating an altimeter

Calibrating an altimeter consists of manually adjusting the elevation reading so that it conforms to your actual elevation. Both mechanical and electronic altimeters are equipped with a calibration mechanism that lets you manually adjust the elevation reading.

To calibrate an altimeter, you must be at a known elevation such as sea level or a surveyed height. You can also adjust your altimeter to a GPS elevation reading. A generally less accurate method is to pinpoint your horizontal location on a topographic map and then adjust your altimeter to the elevation of the nearest contour line. The easiest way to pinpoint your horizontal location on the map is of course with a GPS receiver.

Many unpredictable factors affect an altimeter's elevation reading. To keep your altimeter as accurate as possible, calibrate your altimeter whenever you come across a point of known elevation.

3.3 Factors affecting altimeter accuracy

An altimeter measures the ambient air pressure and then calculates its elevation according to a standard pressure gradient, which is in turn based on average atmospheric conditions. The conditions in the real atmosphere are however rarely average. Air temperature, weather systems, and humidity can alter the pressure gradient and consequently your elevation reading. The temperature of the altimeter itself can also distort the elevation reading.

Air temperature

As air cools, it becomes denser and gravity pulls it closer to the ground. If you are above or inside a layer of cold air, less air remains above you than if the air temperature was normal. The air pressure would therefore be lower than normal for your elevation. The reverse happens if you are above or inside a layer of hot air. More air remains overhead, leading to higher than normal air pressure. There is however no change in the air pressure below a layer of hot or cold air. For example, the air pressure at sea level is not affected by air temperature because all the air is overhead at sea level, regardless of its temperature. As a result, the air pressure changes more rapidly with elevation in cold air than in hot air. In other words, the pressure gradient is steeper in cold air than in hot air.

To calculate its elevation, your altimeter uses a pressure gradient that is based on a standard temperature profile of the atmosphere. In cold air, the real pressure gradient is steeper than the gradient used by your altimeter. Your altimeter reading will therefore change more rapidly than your actual elevation when you ascend or descend through a layer of cold air. In hot air, your altimeter reading will change less rapidly than your actual elevation. If you calibrate your altimeter below or inside a mass of cold air, the altimeter will progressively overestimate its elevation as you ascend through the cold air. Conversely, if you calibrate your altimeter above or inside the same mass of cold air, your altimeter will progressively underestimate its elevation as you descend through the cold air. In hot air, your altimeter will underestimate its elevation during the ascent and overestimate it during the descent, assuming it was calibrated in the same manner. See Table 3.3 for examples.

Table 3.3
Example of altimeter readings inside a layer of hot or cold air stretching from sea level up to 2000 m with various calibration elevations

Actual elevation	Calibrated at 0 m		Calibrated at 1000 m		Calibrated at 2000 m	
	Cold air	Hot air	Cold air	Hot air	Cold air	Hot air
0 m	0 m	0 m	-44 m	41 m	-106 m	104 m
1000 m	1044 m	959 m	1000 m	1000 m	938 m	1063 m
2000 m	2106 m	1896 m	2062 m	1937 m	2000 m	2000 m

To automatically compensate for air temperature, your altimeter would have to know the average temperature of the underlying air and use that information to select an appropriate pressure gradient. Such altimeters do not exist. The only realistic way to compensate for air temperature would be for the user to select a pressure gradient based on the estimated average temperature of the underlying air. Most altimeters, however, do not have this capability.

Humidity

When air absorbs water vapor, the water molecules displace nitrogen and oxygen molecules, the main components of air. This decreases the average air density because water molecules have lower mass than both nitrogen and oxygen molecules. The pressure gradient is therefore less steep in humid air than in dry air. Humidity has a similar effect on your altimeter reading as air temperature, with humid air equivalent to hot air, and dry air equivalent to cold air. To visualize the effect of humidity, look at Table 3.3 and substitute dry for cold, and humid for hot. Altimeter errors caused by humidity are generally less significant than errors caused by air temperature.

To complicate things, hot air can absorb much more water than cold air. This means that the effects of air temperature and humidity will augment each other in hot, humid conditions, and also in cold, dry conditions. For example, an altimeter calibrated at sea level would almost certainly read too low on a summit in a tropical jungle, and too high on an Antarctic summit.

Weather systems

The elevation readings of both mechanical and electronic altimeters are affected by high and low-pressure weather systems that cause the sea-level air pressure to change. At higher elevations, the air pressure usually rises and falls together with the sea-level air pressure of a nearby location. If you stay at one location while a low-pressure system moves in, your altimeter will show a rising elevation even though you haven't moved. Conversely, if a high-pressure system builds up while you're stationary, the elevation reading on your altimeter will drop. Weather change is a common and significant cause of altimeter inaccuracy.

Altimeter temperature

The temperature of the altimeter itself can affect its reading. A change in the temperature of a mechanical altimeter causes the sealed metal chamber and the linkage to expand or contract, thereby moving the needle without any change in air pressure. With electronic altimeters, a change in temperature deforms the piezoresistive sensor and leads to a distorted elevation reading.

Try keeping the temperature of your altimeter as constant as possible since its last calibration. This may be difficult in practice. If you strap the altimeter to your wrist, a change in the temperature of your skin will heat or cool the altimeter. If you leave the altimeter hanging outside, a change in air temperature or radiated heat will alter the altimeter temperature. A sensible compromise is to carry the altimeter in a layer of clothing between your skin and the outside environment. Altimeters with built-in temperature compensation systems will partially mitigate the effect of altimeter temperature.

3.4 Triangulating with altimeter and compass

On reasonably steep terrain, you can triangulate your position with one elevation reading and one field bearing off a landmark. This process is similar to triangulating along a linear feature, but with a contour line substituting for the linear feature. You need a topographic map, a compass, and an altimeter.

1. Take a field bearing off an identifiable landmark. Be sure to compensate for the declination relative to grid north.
2. Place the compass on the map with a corner of the base plate on the landmark.

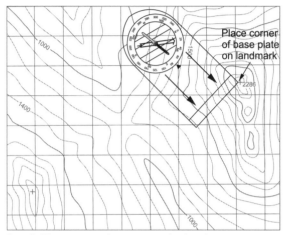

Step 2: Place corner of compass on landmark

3. Using the corner of the base plate as a pivot point, rotate the whole compass until the meridian lines on the compass are parallel to the north-south grid lines on the map. Make sure the compass is oriented so that north (0°) on the graduated dial points toward north on the map, not south.
4. Draw a straight line across the map, parallel to the compass base plate, and through the landmark. This is your first line of position.

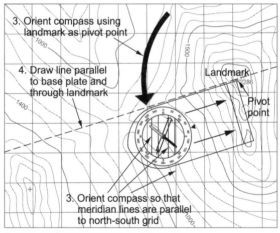

Step 3 - 4: Orient compass and draw line

5. Note the elevation given by your altimeter. Your second line of position is a contour line near your presumed location that matches your altimeter reading.

6. You are located at the intersection between the two lines of position, or in other words, where the compass line of position intersects a contour line that matches your elevation. If there is more than one possible intersection point, investigate the surrounding terrain to narrow your choices down to one. In this case, you have two possible locations, A or B. You can use several methods to narrow the choices down to one. For example, check the slope in the direction of the landmark. If the initial part of the slope is downward, you are at location A, if it's upward you are at location B. Alternatively, use terrain association (Section 8.1) to eliminate one of the choices, or take a field bearing off a second landmark.

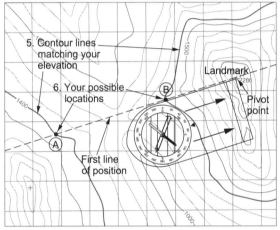

Step 5 - 6: Find contour lines matching your elevation

3.5 Estimating your location by steepest slope

This method is more difficult and less accurate than taking a field bearing off a landmark, and only works in certain types of topography. You need a topographic map, a compass, and an altimeter.

1. Note the elevation given by your altimeter. Your first line of position is a contour line near your presumed location that matches your elevation.

2. Take a field bearing in the direction of the steepest slope (fall line) at your location. Use the same method as for taking a field bearing off a landmark, but point the compass down the fall line instead of toward a landmark. The fall line is the path that a ball would follow if it rolled down the slope. Be sure to compensate for the declination relative to grid north.

3. Place the compass somewhere on the contour line that matches the elevation reading from your altimeter.

4. Orient the compass so that the meridian lines on the compass are parallel with the north-south grid lines on the map. Make sure that the compass is oriented so that north (0°) on the graduated dial points toward north on the map, not south.

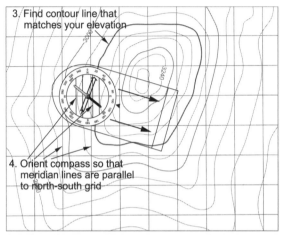

Step 3 - 4: Place compass on contour line and orient compass

5. Without changing its orientation, move the compass along the contour line until the travel direction arrows point down the fall line. One edge of the base plate should be perpendicular to a series of adjacent contour lines. Double check that the meridian lines on the compass are still parallel with the north-south grid. Your location is where the edge of the base plate intersects with the contour line that matches your altimeter reading.

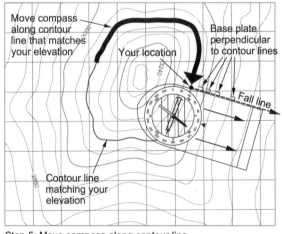

Step 5: Move compass along contour line

Estimating your position by steepest slope has serious limitations, and is usually done only in poor visibility where regular triangulation will not work. It would, for example, be impossible to pinpoint your position if the contour lines were straight near your location. You could be anywhere along the straight contour lines. Even with curved contour lines, you may find several points where the base plate is perpendicular to the contour lines.

If you are unable to pinpoint your location with this method, consider either moving to a location where the topography is more favorable, or waiting for the weather to clear.

Chapter 4
Global Positioning System

A global positioning system (GPS) consists of GPS satellites, associated ground monitoring stations, and individual GPS receivers. By triangulating radio signals transmitted from several GPS satellites, a GPS receiver can automatically compute and display its horizontal position, elevation, direction of travel, speed, and other related information. Several global positioning systems have been, or are being, deployed. The most widely-used one is described here.

4.1 How GPS works

A constellation of GPS satellites has been launched into orbit around Earth. The number varies, but there are normally at least 24 satellites in operation. In the standard configuration, the satellites are arranged into six equally-spaced orbits with four equidistant satellites in each orbit. All orbits are about 20 000 km above Earth's surface and tilted 55° to the equatorial plane. This setup ensures that at least six GPS satellites are overhead anywhere on Earth at any one time. Each satellite completes one orbit in about 12 hours. Ground stations constantly monitor the exact position, speed, and direction of each satellite. This orbit data together with signal timing information is relayed through each satellite to your GPS receiver via a carrier frequency.

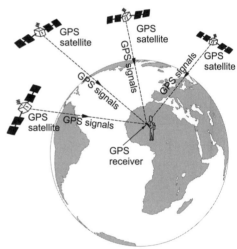

Global positioning system

In addition to the orbit and timing data, each satellite transmits its own unique signature signal toward Earth. Signature signals are transmitted from all GPS satellites at frequent intervals and precise times measured by onboard atomic clocks. By generating equivalent signals in its internal circuit, your GPS receiver can recognize an external signature signal as coming from a particular satellite.

From the orbit and timing data, the receiver knows the location of all the satellites and the exact time when each signature signal was transmitted. Since the signals travel at the speed of light, a known speed, your receiver can use the time differences between the transmitted and received signals to calculate its distance to each satellite. Once the distances to a sufficient number of satellites are known, the receiver uses standard geometric formulas to triangulate its position.

In theory, your receiver needs to know its distance to at least three satellites to triangulate its position in three dimensions. In practice, there is a complicating factor. Your GPS receiver is equipped with a regular quartz clock, not an atomic clock, and cannot directly measure the arrival times of each signature signal with sufficient accuracy. The receiver is however capable of accurately measuring the phase shift between a satellite signal and the corresponding internally generated signal. The phase shift is proportional to the signal travel time from the satellite plus an unknown time offset. This offset is the same for all satellite signals and adds one more unknown term to the geometric formulas needed to calculate the position. The signature signals from one extra satellite will solve this unknown term. Your GPS receiver therefore needs signals from at least four satellites to calculate its position in three dimensions (latitude, longitude, and elevation).

A receiver recalculates its position at regular intervals. A moving receiver that is switched on can compare its current position with previous positions and track any changes. This enables the receiver to compute its speed and direction of travel.

4.2 Causes of GPS position errors

The global positioning system is afflicted by many technical problems and uncontrollable natural phenomena that affect the accuracy of a GPS position fix. A worst-case scenario would be if your GPS receiver broke down or the whole GPS system stopped working. Some less severe but common causes of position error are discussed below.

Atmospheric conditions

Before reaching your GPS receiver, the satellite signals are slowed by charged particles in the ionosphere, the upper portion of Earth's atmosphere. The ensuing time delay is proportional to the number of charged particles that the signal encounters. Air molecules and water vapor also reduce the speed of the satellite signals, mostly in the troposphere, the lower portion of Earth's atmosphere. Your receiver compensates for the signal delay based on a standard model of the atmosphere. The position error will be larger whenever the conditions in the real atmosphere differ from the standard model. For example, the position error will increase during a solar storm because of the dramatic change in the number of charged particles in the ionosphere. The position error is typically a few meters due to conditions in the ionosphere and up to 1 meter because of conditions in the troposphere.

Multipath reflection

Satellite signals may bounce off features such as rock faces before reaching your receiver. The bounced signal can either be mistaken for, or interfere, with the direct signal, introducing something called a multipath reflection error. Because the bounced signal arrives slightly later than the direct signal, some GPS receivers can tell the signals apart and correct the error. The position error caused by multipath reflection is normally less than 1 meter.

Satellite clock errors

Even though the atomic clocks in the satellites are extremely accurate, they are not perfect. Time discrepancies in the atomic clocks can translate into a position error of up to 1 meter.

Satellite orbit errors

Ground stations regularly track the orbital positions of the GPS satellites. If a satellite drifts from its intended orbit, the ground stations detect the error and then update the satellite's orbit data. The position error could be a few meters during the time interval before your receiver is informed about the updated orbit.

Malfunctioning satellites

Occasionally, a GPS satellite may malfunction and transmit inaccurate data. The ground stations normally detect this type of problem within a few minutes and promptly transmit a system status message to all the GPS satellites, which in turn tell your GPS receiver to disregard the signals from the broken satellite. A damaged satellite could cause a large position error before your receiver is informed of its condition.

Deliberate signal degradation

The people who operate the global positioning system are able to deliberately degrade the timing of the signature signals to selected parts of the world. A less accurate position reading in that region would result. The position error can be made arbitrarily large.

Satellite distribution

Because of the inherent constraints of geometry, the distribution of the visible satellites affects the accuracy of your position. Ideally, all the visible satellites should be evenly spaced across the sky. In practice, the satellites are never perfectly distributed. The position accuracy degrades in proportion to how close the visible satellites are clustered together.

Signal obstructions

Obstructions such as trees or adjoining terrain that block the satellite signals are the most common cause of position errors or inability to get a position fix. The greater the number of satellite signals that reach your receiver and the stronger the satellite signals, the better the accuracy. Most receivers attempt to calculate a two-dimensional position fix after obtaining signals from just three satellites. The receiver does this by assuming that it is at a known elevation, usually sea level or the elevation of its last position fix. If the assumed elevation is significantly wrong, the calculated two-dimensional position could be off by a kilometer or more. Manually inserting the correct elevation into the receiver will alleviate this problem.

4.3 Differential GPS (DGPS)

Because the GPS satellites orbit high above Earth, two GPS receivers that are fairly close together will acquire signals that have traveled through roughly the same part of the atmosphere. Errors in signal travel times due to atmospheric conditions and deliberate signal degradation are about the same for both receivers. Both receivers collect exactly the same atomic clock errors and satellite orbit inaccuracies.

A differential global positioning system (DGPS) consists of an accurately surveyed ground station equipped with a reference GPS receiver and a transmitter. The reference receiver continually monitors the arrival times of the signature signals, and compares the arrival times to what they should be to conform to the receiver's known surveyed position. The differences between the actual and expected arrival times of the signals are broadcast as correction signals via the ground station's transmitter.

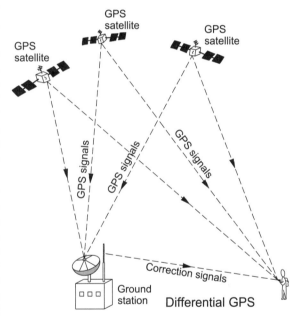

In most cases, any suitably equipped GPS receiver within range of a ground station (typically a few 100 km) can use the correction signals to reduce its position error. Because the ground station does not know which satellite signals your GPS receiver is using for its position fix, it sends you the correction signals for all the satellites overhead. Your receiver only exploits the correction signals from the satellites that are used for your position fix. A receiver located within the range of two or more ground stations typically chooses the correction signals from the base station with the best strength-to-noise ratio of the signals.

DGPS can virtually eliminate satellite orbit and clock errors and greatly reduce errors caused by atmospheric conditions, deliberate signal degradation, and malfunctioning GPS satellites. The resulting position is reliable and typically accurate within a few meters.

4.4 Space-based augmentation systems

Space-based augmentation systems work on principles similar to DGPS. Correction signals are sent from a network of ground stations to a master ground station that transforms the signals into a grid of correction signals. The grid is sent to one or more geostationary satellites that orbit 36 000 km above the equator, and is then broadcast to Earth. The broadcast area is large, often the size of a continent.

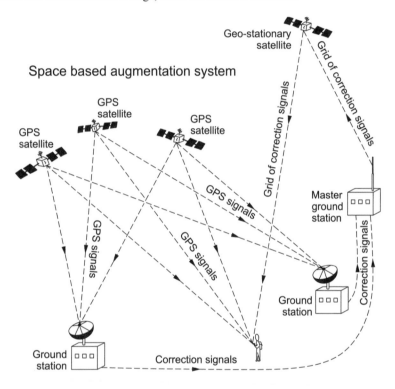

Any suitably equipped receiver within the broadcast area can obtain the complete grid of correction signals. Based on its position within the grid, the receiver interpolates the correction signals from nearby grid points into a set of custom correction signals. The position accuracy is slightly better than for DGPS but can easily be degraded by obstructions that prevent the correction signals from reaching the receiver. Because of their orbits above the equator, the geostationary satellites appear lower on the horizon as you move away from the equator. The grid of correction signals is therefore more likely to be blocked by terrain features at higher latitudes. Pointing your receiver's antenna directly toward the geostationary satellite may improve the position accuracy. The space-based augmentation system itself can of course malfunction and transmit an incorrect correction grid.

4.5 GPS receivers

GPS technology is continually evolving with a large variety of GPS receivers being developed for many types of applications. A GPS receiver can be combined with other electronic devices into one package. Units are available that combine a receiver with an electronic compass, pressure altimeter, wireless phone, or emergency transmitter. Of most interest to wilderness navigators, are lightweight units that can quickly acquire a position fix without consuming too much battery power.

4.5.1 Signal gathering techniques

The method that a GPS receiver uses to gather and process satellite signals governs how quickly and accurately it can obtain a position fix.

Sequential receiver

A sequential receiver uses one channel to gather all the data it needs from one satellite, then switches to the next satellite and so on until it has enough information for a position fix. This type of receiver can get stuck on one satellite if it's unable to obtain a complete signal. The unit is cheap and doesn't use much battery power. However, it is often slow getting a position fix and can quickly lose the fix if a satellite disappears from view.

Multiplexing receiver

Multiplexing receivers use one channel to gather partial data from one satellite for a short time interval, then switch to the next satellite for the same time interval, and so on until there is enough information for a position fix. Multiplexing receivers don't get stuck on one satellite and perform somewhat better than sequential receivers.

Parallel channel receiver

Parallel channel receivers use several separate channels that simultaneously gather signals. Each channel gathers signals from one satellite only. Generally, this type of receiver is faster at getting a position fix, less likely to lose one, and the best type for obtaining position readings under tree cover. The added circuitry uses more battery power. Parallel channel receivers have largely made sequential, multiplexing, and hybrid receivers obsolete.

Hybrid receiver

Hybrid receivers have several separate channels, some of which may be dedicated to a single satellite and some multiplexing or sequential. These types of receivers have intermediate performances.

Dual frequency receiver

Dual frequency receivers are mainly used for surveying or military purposes. They make use of a second carrier frequency transmitted by the GPS satellites to reduce errors caused by atmospheric conditions. These errors can be calculated directly because different frequencies are slowed down by different amounts in the atmosphere. Dual frequency receivers are much more accurate than standard receivers but are heavier and more expensive.

4.5.2 Features that can improve accuracy

Under certain conditions, built-in or optional features can enhance the performance of a GPS receiver.

Correction signal enabled receivers

Receivers that are designed to accept correction signals from differential GPS or space-based augmentation systems can improve the accuracy of a position fix. The receiver must be within a certain radius of an operational ground station to derive any benefit, regardless whether the correction signals arrive via a satellite or directly from a ground station. If your receiver is too far from a ground station, the correction signals may not be relevant for your area.

External antennas

Powered external antennas can be connected to some receivers. These types of antennas amplify weak satellite signals and enhance your receiver's ability to get a position fix under tree cover. Extra battery power is needed to operate the antenna.

Position averaging

Some receivers have a built-in position averaging feature that can improve the accuracy of a waypoint, which is a position fix stored in the receiver's memory. For this feature to work, the receiver must be stationary for a period of time before storing the waypoint. A receiver that is switched on will repeatedly recalculate its position, allowing the software to work out the average of all the previously calculated position fixes. The longer the receiver stays switched on, the more position fixes are available for averaging and the more accurate the subsequently stored waypoint.

4.6 Essential applications for GPS receivers

GPS receivers are designed with many built-in features but only a few are essential for wilderness navigation. Any feature that requires the receiver to stay switched on for prolonged periods should be used sparingly as conserving battery power is an important consideration, especially in cold weather.

Determining your position

The ability to pinpoint your position during any type of weather almost anywhere on Earth is the most basic application of a GPS receiver. Just switch on the receiver and wait for a position fix. Your position can be displayed as a grid number, a geographic coordinate, or a point on a built-in digital map. With signals from a minimum of four satellites, the receiver will display your elevation.

Storing a position as a waypoint

A waypoint is simply a named set of coordinates representing a position. Once your receiver has acquired a position fix, you can store the position in the receiver's memory as a waypoint. This is very useful for finding your way back to the position. You could also give the waypoint's coordinates to someone else, who could then find the waypoint with his or her own receiver.

Inserting a waypoint

You can manually key a position into your receiver's memory as a waypoint without ever having set foot at that location. The coordinates for the waypoint could be obtained from a printed map or from someone else who has previously been there. With a computer, you can insert waypoints electronically into a GPS receiver from a digital map.

Navigating toward a waypoint

Finding your way toward a stored waypoint is the essence of GPS navigation. With waypoints stored in its memory, switch on the receiver and let it acquire a position fix. With a few keystrokes, the receiver will display the distance and bearing toward any stored waypoint. There are two primary ways to navigate toward a stored waypoint: (1) using the receiver by itself, or (2) using it together with a compass. By itself, the receiver must continuously be switched on. With a compass, the receiver requires only intermittent use with most of the navigating done by the compass.

Creating a route from waypoints

This involves organizing stored waypoints into an electronic route with the intention of navigating toward each waypoint in sequence, one after the other.

Plotting and following an electronic trail

When plotting an electronic trail, the GPS receiver automatically saves waypoints at regular intervals as you travel, resulting in a sequence of closely spaced waypoints. When following an electronic trail, the receiver automatically directs you toward the next waypoint along the electronic trail. The receiver must obviously stay switched on while plotting or following an electronic trail.

Calculating distances and bearings

GPS receivers can display the straight-line distance and bearing from your current position to any stored waypoint, or between any two stored waypoints. This is useful for planning routes or checking your progress.

Zeroing-in on a waypoint

Zeroing-in on a waypoint requires pushing the receiver to its limit of accuracy. It's mainly used for finding stashes, snow caves, or other objects hidden by terrain or during very poor visibility.

Getting accurate time

The time on the receiver's quartz clock is obtained from the satellite signals and cannot be adjusted manually. The signal from one satellite is sufficient to set the time on your receiver to within one millisecond. This does not necessarily mean that your receiver accurately resets its quartz clock as soon as it gets a signal from one satellite. The clocks on the GPS satellites are set to something called GPS time, which is offset from universal time by several seconds. The offset changes because leap seconds are periodically added to universal time but not to GPS time. The offset is broadcast from the satellites to the receiver once every few minutes. The receiver's clock may be off by several seconds before it has obtained the offset from the satellites. If a receiver has been switched off for a prolonged period, the time shown on the receiver is only as accurate as the internal quartz clock and could be off by several minutes.

4.7 GPS receiver basic use

Before heading into the wilderness, read your receiver's instruction manual and learn how to use some key features. Aside from a GPS receiver, you will need a compass and a map of your area.

Indoor preparation

Try the following while you are indoors:

- Switch on your GPS receiver and immediately disable the satellite signal-acquiring system. Otherwise, the receiver will begin a futile struggle trying to get a position fix indoors.

- Adjust the time offset to show the local time for your area. You need to add or subtract a certain number of hours from the default setting of universal time. The time itself cannot be adjusted because it is acquired from the satellite signals.

- Find out how to switch between magnetic, true, and grid bearings. Select true or grid bearings if your compass has an adjustable declination mechanism. If not, it may be easier to use magnetic bearings.

- Select your preferred units of measure. It is easier to navigate when your GPS receiver is set to the same units as your map.

- Select a horizontal map datum. The horizontal datum in your receiver must correspond to the datum that is marked on your map. If your receiver allows, select a vertical datum that matches the one used by your map.

- Select an appropriate coordinate system, either geographic coordinates or a specific grid. Choose the same grid as the one on your map. If there's no grid on your map, select geographic coordinates.

- Enter waypoints for nearby locations into your receiver. This can be done manually from a paper map or electronically from a digital map (Section 4.8).

- Arrange several stored waypoints into an electronic route. Check the straight-line distances and bearings between adjacent waypoints and the total travel distance of the route. Practice inserting new waypoints into the route as well as removing old waypoints.

Outdoor practice

Go outside and switch on the receiver. Make sure the satellite signal-acquiring system is enabled.

- If the GPS receiver has never been used before or has moved a large distance since its previous position fix, you may need to initialize the receiver for your region. This involves selecting the country or region where the receiver is located. If you don't initialize the receiver, it may take a long time to get the first position fix, or you may not be able to acquire one.

- Observe the receiver's screen as it acquires satellite signals. Some receivers show the relative positions of the overhead satellites and the strengths of the incoming signals. After acquiring a position fix, the receiver may give you an estimated position error. The real error in your position could be much larger because the receiver doesn't know all the factors that affect its calculated position.

- Save the position fix as a waypoint and give it a descriptive name.

- Pinpoint the GPS-acquired position on your map by using the map's grid or geographic coordinates.

- Make the receiver display the distance and bearing from your current position to a nearby, previously stored waypoint. Set the graduated dial of your compass to this bearing and then follow the bearing to the waypoint. If you do not have a compass, use the receiver's direction arrow or its built-in electronic compass to guide you to the waypoint. GPS receivers usually have several schemes for navigating toward a waypoint.

- After reaching the waypoint, use the receiver and compass to navigate back toward your original position. As you approach your original position, use the receiver to zero-in as close as possible to your original saved waypoint (Section 4.9).

- Plot an electronic trail by traveling at a steady pace while the receiver is switched on. The result is usually shown as a curved line on the receiver's display.

- Use your GPS receiver to guide you back along the same electronic route to your starting point. This process requires some practice to master.

If you can do the above, you will know enough to exploit the navigation power of the GPS.

4.8 Entering waypoints into a GPS receiver

You can manually insert waypoints into your GPS receiver from paper maps, or use a computer to insert the waypoints from a digital map.

4.8.1 Manual transfer of waypoints from map to receiver

You will need a GPS receiver and a map with grid lines or geographic coordinate lines drawn across the map. Be careful when entering the numbers into your receiver. Wrong numbers can lead to serious navigation errors.

1. On the map, plot your anticipated route as a series of straight-line segments. Mark the intersections between segments as waypoints.

2. Look for the map datum written somewhere in the margins of your map. Switch on your receiver and adjust its horizontal datum to correspond with the one on the map.

3. Check the margins of your map to determine what grid system it uses. Set your receiver to display the same grid as the one used by your map. If your map doesn't have a grid, use geographic coordinates.

4. Determine the grid numbers (easting and northing) or geographic coordinates (latitude and longitude) of your waypoints and manually key them into your receiver. Label the waypoints in your receiver and arrange them sequentially into a route. Double-check your numbers.

Example of inserting waypoints

After analyzing the contour lines on the map below, you plot a route from your current position (A) via intermediate waypoints (B) through (E) to your destination (F).

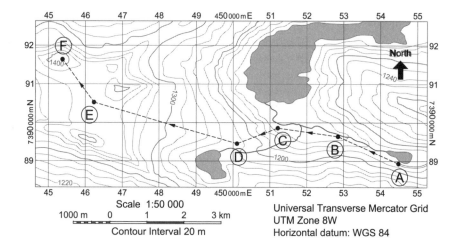

Scale 1:50 000

1000 m 0 1 2 3 km

Contour Interval 20 m

Universal Transverse Mercator Grid
UTM Zone 8W
Horizontal datum: WGS 84

Your map shows that it uses the 1984 World Geodetic System datum (WGS 84). Set the horizontal datum in your receiver to WGS 84. The map also shows that it uses the universal transverse Mercator (UTM) grid. Set your receiver to display positions in the UTM/UPS grid system. The UTM zone is given as 8W and applies to all the waypoints on this map.

On your map, each grid square represents 1000 m x 1000 m. You should be able to visually estimate the easting and northing of each waypoint to within one tenth of a square or 100 m. After determining the easting and northing of a waypoint (Section 1.6.3), enter the numbers into your GPS receiver. The numbers corresponding to each waypoint are shown below:

(A): Zone 8W, easting = 454 500 m E, northing = 7 388 900 m N
(B): Zone 8W, easting = 452 800 m E, northing = 7 389 600 m N
(C): Zone 8W, easting = 451 200 m E, northing = 7 389 900 m N
(D): Zone 8W, easting = 450 100 m E, northing = 7 389 500 m N
(E): Zone 8W, easting = 446 200 m E, northing = 7 390 500 m N
(E): Zone 8W, easting = 445 400 m E, northing = 7 391 600 m N

Arrange these waypoints sequentially into an electronic route in your receiver.

4.8.2 Electronic transfer of waypoints into GPS receiver

With digital maps, waypoints can be inserted into the GPS receiver from a computer. Other than a GPS receiver and a computer, you need a suitable software package, relevant digital maps, and an interface cable.

1. Connect your GPS receiver to the computer with the interface cable.

2. Boot up the computer, start the appropriate software, and download the digital maps.

3. Create waypoints with the program by clicking on selected points on the digital maps. Save the waypoints on the computer.

4. Set the map datum on your receiver to the same datum as the one on the digital map.

5. Transfer the waypoints to the GPS receiver. Check your receiver to make sure the waypoints have in fact been transferred.

4.9 Zeroing-in on a waypoint

During normal navigation, your GPS receiver will usually provide you with better position accuracy than you actually need. Under certain circumstances such as when trying to find a stash or a campsite during a total whiteout, you may want to precisely pinpoint a previously stored waypoint. To do this, take advantage the GPS receiver's distance measuring system and direction arrow or electronic compass.

Receiver with a built-in electronic compass

A GPS receiver with a built-in electronic compass is ideally suited for zeroing-in on a waypoint.

1. Switch on the receiver, wait for a position fix, and make the receiver show the bearing to the selected waypoint as an arrow. Make sure that the displayed arrow is derived from the electronic compass and isn't a direction arrow. The two types of arrows may look similar.

2. Follow the arrow toward the waypoint while watching the displayed distance decrease. Eventually, the displayed distance will start to increase and the arrow will fluctuate wildly. This is probably as close as your GPS receiver can lead you to the waypoint. Stop and mark your position with an object such as a wand or backpack. Do a grid search if necessary.

Receiver without a built-in compass

Don't confuse a GPS receiver's direction arrow with an electronic compass arrow. A direction arrow only works when you're moving. Without a built-in electronic compass, a GPS receiver has no way of knowing which way it is oriented. A moving receiver can however compute its direction of motion relative to the direction to a waypoint, and display the difference as an arrow. If the receiver is oriented in the direction of motion, the direction arrow will eventually point toward the waypoint.

1. Switch on your receiver, wait for a position fix, and make the receiver show the distance and bearing to the selected waypoint. Display the bearing as a direction arrow.

2. Keep the receiver pointed straight ahead while you move forward in a straight line toward the assumed direction of the waypoint. Observe the direction arrow. At first, the arrow will probably point in the wrong direction. For the moment, ignore the arrow and keep moving forward along the same straight line.

3. As you continue moving, the direction arrow will eventually stabilize and point in the correct direction toward your selected waypoint.

4. While moving, slowly change your travel direction until the direction arrow points straight ahead. Follow the direction arrow toward the waypoint. Keep an eye on the displayed distance. It should decrease as you move toward the waypoint. If not, you are headed in the wrong direction.

Step 2:
As you start moving, the direction arrow will probably point in the wrong direction.

Step 3:
After moving in the initial direction for some time, the direction arrow will point toward the waypoint.

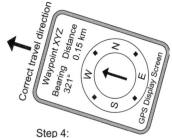

Step 4:
Slowly turn until you're moving in the same direction as the arrow. Follow the direction arrow toward waypoint.

5. Eventually, the displayed distance will start to increase and the direction arrow will fluctuate wildly. This is probably as close as your receiver can lead you to the waypoint. Stop and mark this position. If you haven't found what you are looking for, do a grid search around the marked position to find the exact location.

Chapter 5
Celestial Navigation

From a vantage point on Earth, celestial bodies appear to move across the sky in predictable trajectories. Over the last few thousand years, many techniques have been devised to navigate using the sun, moon, planets, and stars. Celestial navigation is well suited for navigating across oceans, deserts, steppes, tundra, polar ice fields, or any large expanse that lacks obvious landmarks but has horizon-to-horizon visibility. Round-the-clock celestial navigation is possible by switching between celestial bodies that are visible during the day and those that are visible at night. Your navigational potential is governed by what celestial bodies, if any, are visible and what instruments and documentation you have at your disposal:

- With the help of a clock, the sun and moon can be used as rough direction finders.

- With the help of a celestial navigation almanac, you can use the stars to estimate your latitude, and also as rough direction finders.

- With a clock and an almanac, you can estimate your longitude from the stars.

- With the addition of a suitable angle-measuring device such as a sextant, you can use almost any type of celestial body to calculate your position to within a few kilometers.

5.1 Celestial coordinate system

To help pinpoint celestial bodies, a celestial coordinate system has been developed that is based on the same principles as Earth's geographic coordinate system. From Earth's perspective, the celestial bodies appear to be located on the inside surface of an imaginary celestial sphere of indeterminate size. The celestial sphere has two celestial poles located directly above Earth's geographic poles. There is also a celestial equator that is a projection of Earth's equator onto the celestial sphere.

The celestial equivalent to latitude is called the declination (Dec). It is measured in degrees north or south of the celestial equator. "Declination" is an unfortunate term as it can be confused with magnetic declination. The declination is sometimes denoted as a negative number south of the celestial equator.

The celestial equivalent to longitude is called hour angle. Several types of hour angle are used in celestial navigation. The most important one is the Greenwich hour angle (GHA), which is measured in degrees from the Greenwich celestial meridian, the projection of Earth's prime meridian onto the celestial sphere. The GHA is measured westward all the way to 360° so there is no east or west label. Because of Earth's rotation around its axis, the GHA of a celestial body is constantly changing.

The sidereal hour angle (SHA) is a measure of the relative east-west position between bodies on the celestial sphere. It is measured in degrees from a reference meridian called the Aries meridian, the celestial equivalent to Earth's prime meridian. The Aries meridian passes through the spring equinox, the point on the celestial equator that the sun crosses each year around March 21. Like the GHA, the SHA is measured westward all the way to 360°. The SHA is only used when stating the hour angles of stars, and not the sun, moon, or planets. This is because the stars are so incredibly distant from Earth that they don't appear to move relative to each other. The position of the Aries meridian does however change slowly because of the precession and wobble of Earth's axis. There is therefore a gradual change of the SHA for stars from year to year. The local hour angle (LHA) is the angle from the observer's longitude to the celestial meridian of the body. Like other hour angles, it is also measured westward to 360°.

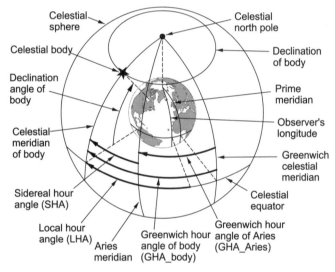

Celestial coordinate system

Celestial navigation almanacs show the declination and hour angles of selected celestial bodies at specific times and dates. The time is always stated as universal time (UT) and the date as universal date (UD). To save space, most almanacs do not directly list the GHA of the stars but instead list the GHA of the Aries meridian and the SHA of the stars. To calculate the GHA of a star, add the GHA of Aries to the SHA of the star. Use the formula: GHA_Aries + SHA = GHA_body

Example of celestial position

You want the celestial coordinates for the star Markab at 18:32:55 (UT) on March 23, 2010 (UD). According to an almanac, the declination for Markab is 15°15.5'N. The Greenwich hour angle for Aries (GHA_Aries) for that time and date is 99°22.2'. The sidereal hour angle (SHA) for Markab is 13°41.0'. The Greenwich hour angle for the body (GHA_body) is therefore 13°41.0' + 99°22.2' = 113°03.2'. The complete position of Markab is written as: Dec 15°15.5'N, GHA 113°03.2'.

5.2 The sun

The sun, being easy to identify and highly visible, is a convenient astronomical body for finding directions. During cloudy weather, the sun's bearing can sometimes be determined by looking for the brightest point in the sky. The sun travels along an arc across the sky that varies with your latitude and the seasons, but is nearly constant from year to year. At mid-latitudes, the sun's bearing can sometimes be estimated with reasonable accuracy by looking at your clock.

5.2.1 Using a clock to find the sun's bearing

From Earth's perspective, the sun completes one circuit across the sky every 24 hours. This works out to a westward movement of 15° per hour. By assuming that the sun is due south at noon in the northern hemisphere (due north in the southern hemisphere), you have a relationship between the sun's bearing and the time of day (Table 5.1). You can then figure out the sun's bearing anytime of the day by looking at your clock and interpolating the table. With a bit of practice you should be able to estimate the sun's bearing without a table.

Table 5.1 Rough bearings of sun at selected times of day		
Time of day	Northern hemisphere	Southern hemisphere
00:00	North (0°)	South(180°)
03:00	Northeast (45°)	Southeast (135°)
06:00	East (90°)	East (90°)
09:00	Southeast (135°)	Northeast (45°)
12:00	South (180°)	North (0°)
15:00	Southwest (225°)	Northwest (315°)
18:00	West (270°)	West (270°)
21:00	Northwest (315°)	Southwest (225°)

Most people are unaware of the inherent limitations of this method. The bearings shown in Table 5.1 can be fairly accurate or significantly incorrect. The underlying causes of the errors are the time zone of the observer, Earth's elliptical orbit around the sun, Earth's axis tilt, and the curvature of Earth's surface. To understand how these factors affect the sun's bearing, the errors have been broken down into three themes: (1) time errors caused by the observer's longitude, (2) annual time errors caused by Earth's elliptical orbit and axis tilt, and (3) daily bearing errors caused by the observer's latitude. A thorough analysis of the last two themes requires advanced trigonometry and only a cursory explanation will be given here. The only sure way to obtain an accurate bearing of the sun is to look up the bearing in a celestial navigation almanac or to use a celestial navigation calculator.

Time errors caused by observer's longitude

Unless the sun is directly overhead, it always points due south or due north when it reaches its highest point in the sky. This happens once a day at the exact moment when the sun crosses your local celestial meridian. To accurately determine the sun's bearing, your clock must read noon when the sun reaches its highest point, but in practice, most clocks are set to the official time in the time zone where the clock is located. The official time in a zone is loosely based on how far east or west the zone is from the prime meridian. In an ideal world, each time zone would cover a swath of territory 15° of longitude wide, but in the real world, the time zones conform to political boundaries. Official times are a certain number of hours ahead or behind universal time, but are sometimes offset by an additional half hour increment. In some jurisdictions, the official time switches between standard time and daylight saving time. Typically, the official time is changed from standard time to daylight saving time by adding one hour in the spring. In the fall, the official time reverts to standard time by subtracting one hour.

Each time zone has a central longitude where the average position of the sun is due south (northern hemisphere) or due north (southern hemisphere) at noon. To calculate the location of your zone's central longitude, find out the time difference between your clock time and universal time, and then multiply the difference in hours by 15°. The central longitude is obviously east if you're in the eastern hemisphere and west if you're in the western hemisphere. For example, if you're in the eastern hemisphere and the official time is 9.5 hours from universal time, the central longitude is 9.5 x 15° = 142.5°E.

If you're located west of the central longitude, subtract 4 minutes from your clock time for each degree you are from the central longitude. If you're east of the central longitude, add 4 minutes to your clock time for each degree. For example, if you're at 133°E and the central longitude is at 142.5°E, you are west of the central longitude by 142.5° - 133° = 9.5°. Subtract 38 minutes from your clock time, the result of 4 minutes multiplied by 9.5. Time errors caused by the observer's longitude become more pronounced at high latitudes where the longitudes converge toward the poles.

Annual time errors caused by Earth's elliptical orbit and axis tilt

After compensating for your longitude, your clock will probably not read exactly noon when the sun reaches its highest point. Only the average position of the sun over a one-year period will be due north or south at noon. This is why universal time was previously known as Greenwich mean (average) time.

Because of Earth's elliptical orbit around the sun, Earth's distance to the sun varies throughout the year. Earth is closest to the sun around January 2 and furthest away around July 3. Earth travels faster along sections where it is closer to the sun and slower when it is further from the sun. This leads to an accumulated time error (Graph 5.2) that is a measure of the sun's actual position compared to where it would be if it moved uniformly. The error can be as much as 7.6 minutes. For example, if the sun is due south at a particular location at 12:00.0 on January 2, it will be due south at 11:52.4 on April 2 and due south at 12:07.6 on October 2.

From Earth's perspective, the sun appears to travel along an annual arc on the celestial sphere called the ecliptic. Because of the tilt of Earth's axis, the ecliptic is tilted by 23.5° with respect to the equatorial plane. When calculating the annual time error due to axis tilt, you're not interested in how fast the sun moves along the ecliptic but rather how fast it moves across the celestial meridians. One way to visualize this is to look at the movement of the sun's projection onto the equatorial plane.

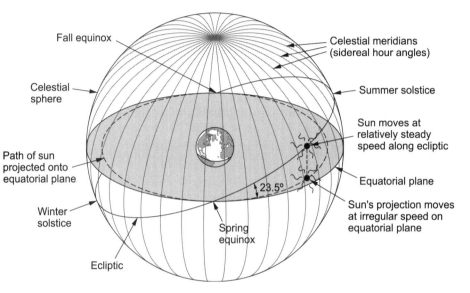

The sun crosses the celestial equator at the spring equinox around March 21, and then begins its journey through parts of the north celestial hemisphere. At the equinox, the sun travels at an angle of 23.5° to the equatorial plane, and only a portion of the sun's movement is projected onto the equatorial plane. At this point, the projected sun moves slower than the actual sun. As the sun moves higher into the north celestial hemisphere, it travels increasingly more parallel to the equatorial plane and the distance between celestial meridians decreases. Both these factors cause the angular speed of the projected sun to increase. At the summer solstice, around June 21, the sun reaches its highest point in the north celestial hemisphere and the projected sun attains its maximum angular speed. After June 21, the projected sun gradually slows down until it crosses into the south celestial hemisphere at the fall equinox around September 22. The cycle is then repeated for the south celestial hemisphere. The irregular angular speed of the sun creates an accumulated time error of up to 9.6 minutes (Graph 5.2). In other words, the axis tilt causes the sun to be due south or due north up to 9.6 minutes before or after noon.

The solid line in Graph 5.2 on the next page shows the combined error caused by both the elliptical orbit and the axis tilt. The combined error varies from 0 to about 16 minutes and is the same for all locations on Earth.

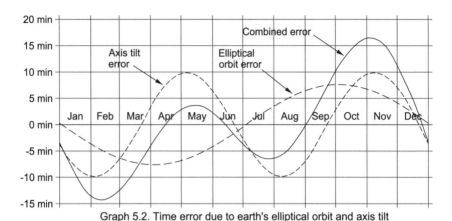

Graph 5.2. Time error due to earth's elliptical orbit and axis tilt

Daily bearing errors caused by observer's latitude

After correcting for your longitude, Earth's elliptical orbit, and Earth's axis tilt, an accurate clock will always read noon when the sun is at its highest point. Away from the tropics, the noon sun will be exactly south in northern hemisphere and exactly north in southern hemisphere. The clock will also read midnight when the sun reaches its lowest point, although this may not be observable. But what about other times of the day? Will the sun be due east at 6:00, for example? In most cases, it will not.

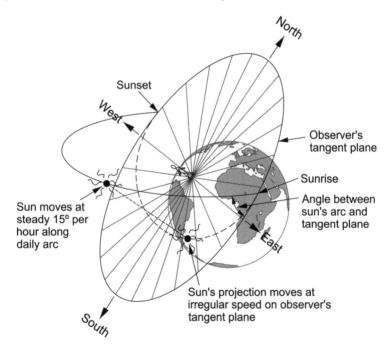

When establishing the sun's bearing, you're actually looking for the direction of the sun projected down onto your tangent plane, which is an extension of your horizon to the celestial sphere. The apparent daily arc of the sun is tilted by a certain angle relative to your tangent plane. This angle changes with the seasons and your latitude. Although the sun moves along its arc at close to a steady 15° per hour, the sun's projection on the tangent plane moves at irregular speed. At sunrise, the sun climbs steeply and only a portion of its movement is projected down to the tangent plane. The angular speed of the projected sun is therefore less than 15° per hour. See illustration on previous page.

As the sun climbs higher in the sky, it travels increasingly more parallel to the tangent plane and the relative distance between the projected sun and the observer decreases. This causes the angular speed of the projected sun to increase. In the middle of the day, the projected sun travels faster than 15° per hour. The projected sun then gradually slows down until sunset. The speed fluctuations lead to a bearing error that varies throughout the day but is always zero at noon and midnight.

The greater the angle between the sun's arc and the observer's horizon, the greater the potential bearing error. The error therefore depends both on the observer's latitude and the time of the year. Only at the geographic poles where the speed of the projected sun is constant, is there never a bearing error. As you move away from the poles, the speed of the projected sun becomes progressively more irregular and the bearing error more significant. To compensate for the bearing error, you need tables or graphs that show the sun's position at every latitude, for every hour of the day, and for every day of the year. A more practical solution for the wilderness traveler is to carry a celestial navigation calculator.

Sun's bearing - Example 1:

Let's say you are traveling through the Gobi Desert in Mongolia (45°N, 102°E), and want to estimate the sun's bearing. It is 16:47 local time on July 18. Mongolia does not use daylight saving time.

Table 5.1 gives the bearing to the sun as roughly west-southwest for this time of the day. Taking into account that the sun moves westward, on average, by one degree every four minutes you can do a more precise interpolation. Your clock is 107 minutes past 15:00, giving you a precisely interpolated but uncorrected bearing of 225° + 107/4 = 252°.

You're in the eastern hemisphere and the official time in Mongolia is 8 hours ahead of universal time. The central longitude for your time zone is therefore 8 x 15° = 120°E. You're located west of the central longitude by 120° - 102° = 18°. Subtracting 4 minutes from your clock time for each degree that you are from the central longitude gives you a corrected time of 16:47 - 18 x 4 min = 15:35.

For July 18, the combined error from Graph 5.2 gives an additional clock error of about -6 minutes. Your new clock time becomes 15:35 - 6 min = 15:29. Your interpolated bearing from Table 5.1 becomes 225° + 29/4 = 232°. This bearing is corrected for your longitude, Earth's axis tilt, and Earth's elliptical orbit.

The graph below was derived from a computer program. It shows the relationship between the time of the day and the bearing error at latitude 45°N on July 18. For a time of 15:29, the graph gives a bearing error of about +26°. Adding this to your bearing gives a new bearing of 232° + 26° = 258°.

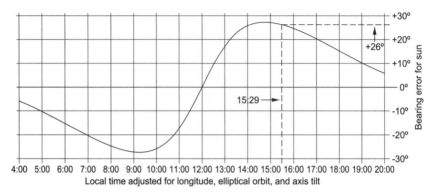

45°N - Bearing error due to latitude - July 18

Comparing this corrected bearing (258°) with the initial uncorrected bearing (252°) gives a total bearing error of only 6°. You were lucky this time! The sun is indeed roughly west-southwest. The large error caused by your longitude was largely compensated by an opposite error due to your latitude. A few hours earlier or later, your uncorrected bearing would have been off by a significant amount.

Sun's bearing - Example 2:

While trekking through northern Bolivia (12°S, 67°W), you want to estimate the sun's bearing. The local time is 10:12 on January 3. Bolivia does not use daylight saving time.

Table 5.1 gives the bearing to the sun as roughly north-northeast. Your clock is 72 minutes past 9:00, giving you a precisely interpolated but uncorrected bearing of 45° - 72/4 = 27°.

You're in the western hemisphere and the official time in Bolivia is 4 hours behind universal time. The central longitude of your time zone is therefore 4 x 15° = 60°W. You're located west of the central longitude by 67° - 60° = 7°. Subtracting 4 minutes from your clock time for each degree that you are from the central longitude gives you a corrected time of 10:12 - 7 x 4 min = 09:44.

For January 3, the combined error from Graph 5.2 gives an additional clock error of about -5 minutes. Your new clock time becomes 09:44 - 5 min = 09:39. Your interpolated bearing from Table 5.1 is then 45° - 39/4 = 35°. This bearing is corrected for your longitude, as well as Earth's axis tilt and elliptical orbit.

The graph on the next page was derived from a computer program. It shows the relationship between the time of the day and the bearing error at latitude 12°S on January 3. For a time of 09:39, the graph gives a bearing error of about +78°. Adding this to your previous corrected bearing gives a new bearing of 35° + 78° = 113°.

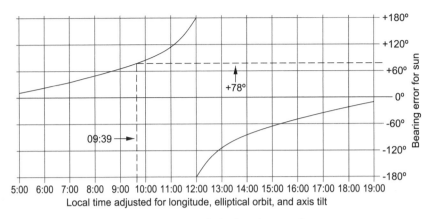

12°S - Bearing error due to latitude - January 3

Comparing the fully corrected bearing (113°) with the initial uncorrected bearing (27°) gives a total bearing error of an astonishing 86°. In other words, the uncorrected bearing will lead you seriously astray. This example clearly illustrates the difficulty in trying to casually estimate the sun's bearing in the tropics (23.5°S - 23.5°N) where the sun is north at noon for part of the year and south for the rest of the year. A sensible technique near the equator is to assume that the sun is roughly east during the morning and roughly west during the afternoon. If the sun is high in the sky, wait for it to move lower before trying to estimate its bearing. The only precise method, of course, is to use a celestial navigation almanac or calculator.

5.2.2 Stick shadow method

There are several variations of the stick shadow method. The one shown here requires that you to start the procedure in the morning and stay with it at least until noon. During the morning, find a patch of level ground and plant a stick vertically into the ground. Mark the end of the stick's shadow. Use a second stick to scribe a circle on the ground, centered on the vertical stick and with a radius the same length as the shadow.

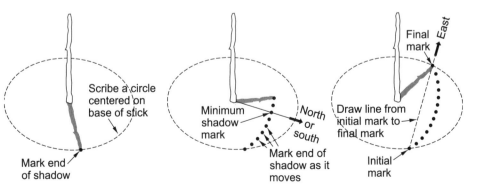

Periodically mark the end of the shadow as it moves. The length of the shadow decreases as the morning progresses until it reaches a minimum at noon and then increases in the afternoon. A line drawn from the base of the stick to the minimum-shadow mark will point north in the northern hemisphere and south in the southern hemisphere. In the tropics, the line will point north for part of the year and south for the rest of the year, depending on your latitude. For a more precise result continue watching and marking the shadow until it crosses the circle that you've scribed on the ground. A line drawn from the initial shadow mark to the final shadow mark will point due east anywhere in the world except at the geographic poles.

The great thing about this method is that you don't have to worry about errors caused by your longitude, latitude, Earth's elliptical orbit, or Earth's axis tilt. All these errors are automatically factored in.

5.3 The moon

The moon's position in the sky at a certain time of day varies daily and is governed by its monthly orbit around Earth. You cannot directly determine the moon's bearing by simply looking at your clock. You can however do it indirectly by observing the moon's phase.

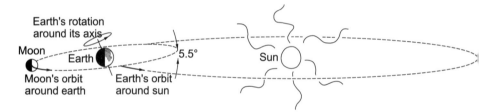

The moon's orbit around Earth is tilted by only about 5.5° relative to Earth's orbit around the sun. For an observer on Earth, this means that the sun and the moon appear to travel along roughly the same arc across the celestial sphere. At any one moment, the sun and moon are a certain angle apart in their perceived mutual arc. This angle can be described as the moon leading or trailing the sun by a certain number of hours.

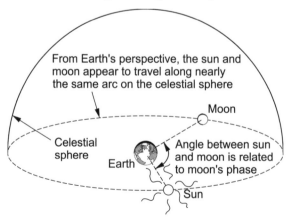

The angle between the sun and the moon is correlated to the moon's phase. For example, a full moon means that the moon is on the opposite side of the arc, and you can think of the full moon as leading or trailing the sun by 12 hours. Whether the moon is leading or trailing is governed by what side of the moon is bright and what hemisphere you're in. For example, a half moon in the southern hemisphere with its bright side to the left means that the moon is trailing the sun by 6 hours.

The relationship between the moon's phase and its relative angle to the sun can be derived from trigonometry. See Table 5.3 for selected results. With a bit of practice, you should be able to just look at the moon to figure out by how many hours it is leading or trailing the sun. Adding or subtracting these hours from your clock time gives you the time when sun will be, or was, where the moon is now. The bearing of the sun at that time is the current bearing of the moon.

Table 5.3 Correlation between moon's phase and relative position to sun		
Phase	Northern hemisphere	Southern hemisphere
◑	opposite sun (12 hours)	opposite sun (12 hours)
◑	leading sun by 10 hours	trailing sun by 10 hours
◑	leading sun by 8 hours	trailing sun by 8 hours
◐	leading sun by 6 hours	trailing sun by 6 hours
◖	leading sun by 4 hours	trailing sun by 4 hours
◖	leading sun by 2 hours	trailing sun by 2 hours
◯	same as sun (0 hours)	same as sun (0 hours)
◗	trailing sun by 2 hours	leading sun by 2 hours
◗	trailing sun by 4 hours	leading sun by 4 hours
◗	trailing sun by 6 hours	leading sun by 6 hours
◑	trailing sun by 8 hours	leading sun by 8 hours
◑	trailing sun by 10 hours	leading sun by 10 hours

5.3.1 Estimating the moon's bearing

The following steps describe how to calculate the moon's bearing. You're essentially using the sun's bearing to figure out the moon's bearing. All the errors that apply to the sun's bearing will therefore carry over to the moon's bearing. There is also the additional error from estimating the moon's phase.

1. Look at the moon and figure out if it is leading or trailing the sun. In the northern hemisphere, the moon is trailing the sun if the bright part of the moon is facing right, and leading if it is facing left. In the southern hemisphere the opposite is true, a right facing bright side means the moon is leading the sun and left facing bright side means it's trailing the sun. In the tropics, the bright side of the moon may be facing up or down rather than left or right, making it difficult to figure out if it is leading or trailing the sun.

2. Determine by approximately how many hours the moon is leading or trailing the sun by looking at the moon's phase (Table 5.3). Interpolate the table for intermediate phases. Subtract the number of hours from your current time if the moon is trailing and add the number of hours if the moon is leading.

3. Determine where the sun's bearing was/will be at this adjusted time. This is the current bearing of the moon.

A more accurate method is to calculate the moon's bearing directly by using a celestial navigation almanac or a calculator. The almanac or calculator gives you the moon's bearing with inputs of your latitude, longitude, local time, local date, and time offset from universal time.

Moon's bearing - Example 1:

You're traveling in east-central Australia (26°S, 144°E), on July 16, 2009. At 04:16 local time the moon looks like the illustration on the left.

A half moon in the southern hemisphere with its bright side facing right means that the moon is leading the sun by 6 hours (Table 5.3). The moon is therefore where the sun will be 6 hours later at 10:16. A rough estimate of the sun's bearing at 10:16 puts it toward the north-northeast (Table 5.1). This is the approximate bearing of the moon. Interpolating Table 5.1 gives a precise but uncorrected bearing of 45° - 76/4 = 26°.

Plugging your latitude (26°S), longitude (144°E), local time (04:16), local date (July 16, 2009), and time offset from universal time (+10 hours) into a celestial navigation calculator gives a bearing of 40°. The moon is actually closer to the northeast than north-northeast. Your estimated bearing is off by 14°, good enough for rough direction finding.

Moon's bearing - Example 2:

You're in southern Greenland (62°N, 45°W), on March 29, 2005. At 02:54 local time the moon looks like the illustration on the left.

Just a few days earlier, Greenland switched to daylight saving time by adding one hour to the local time. Subtract one hour to convert to standard time (01:54). Being in the northern hemisphere, the moon's phase shows that it is leading the sun by roughly 10 hours (Table 5.3). The moon is where the sun will be in 10 hours, at 11:54. At that time, the sun's bearing will be almost exactly south (Table 5.1). Interpolating Table 5.1 gives a precise but uncorrected bearing of 180° - 6/4 = 179°.

Plugging your latitude (62°S), longitude (45°W), local time (02:54), local date (March 29, 2005), and time offset from universal time (-2 hours, for daylight saving time) into a celestial navigation calculator gives a bearing of 170°. Your estimated bearing is off by only 9°, a good approximation of the moon's actual bearing.

5.4 Stars

Because of their great distances from Earth, stars don't appear to change position relative to each other, and star patterns, called constellations, look almost the same today as they did hundreds of years ago. From our perspective on Earth, each star appears permanently fixed to a particular position on the rotating celestial sphere. At the equator, all stars on the celestial sphere rise and set. At the poles, only half the stars on the celestial sphere are visible but these stars never rise nor set. At intermediate latitudes, some stars rise and set while others are always above or always below the horizon.

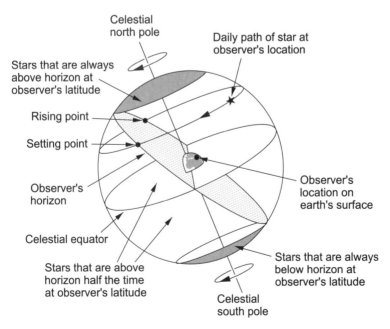

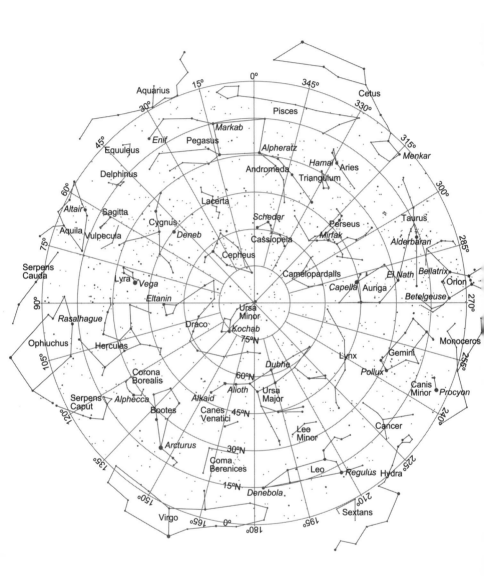

North celestial hemisphere

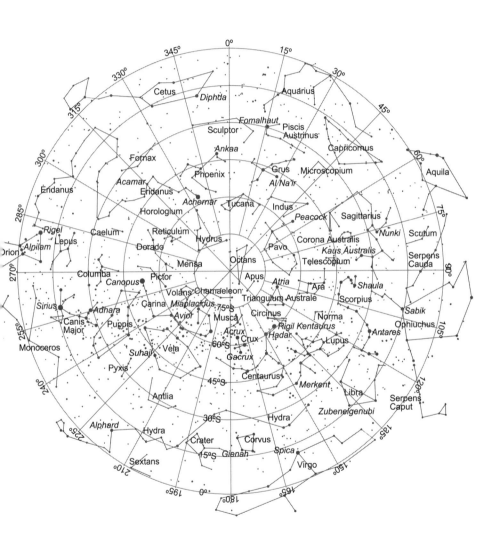

South celestial hemisphere

At a fixed location on Earth, a particular rising-setting star always rises at the same point on the eastern horizon, follows the same arc across the sky, and sets at the same point on the western horizon. This is true throughout the year, although the stars rise and set four minutes earlier each day. This means that at certain times of the year, some stars are above the horizon during daylight hours and therefore invisible.

Before trying to navigate with stars, familiarize yourself with the night sky. Study star charts such as the ones on the previous two pages to learn where the important stars are located. A star chart is similar to a map except that you're looking up instead of down and celestial coordinates are used instead of geographical coordinates. Like maps, star charts are created using various types of projections.

Most bright stars belong to a particular constellation. The easiest way to identify a star is to first find its constellation and then determine the star's position within the constellation. To determine a star's declination (latitude) and sidereal hour angle (longitude), look at a star chart or look up the numbers in an almanac.

The consistent movement and abundant numbers of stars make them inherently well suited for navigation. The biggest drawback is that navigational information can be extracted from stars in so many ways that the task can seem overwhelming. There are two main navigation applications for stars: (1) finding a particular bearing, and (2) determining your location.

5.4.1 Finding north or south

Earth's axis of rotation points to two distinct positions in the sky, the north and south celestial poles. These two positions are essentially long-distance landmarks. A bright star located very near the north celestial pole makes this position in the sky easy to identify. Unfortunately, there is no corresponding bright star near the south celestial pole.

Finding due north

A bright star called Polaris is located within 1° of the north celestial pole in the constellation Ursa Minor, also known as the Little Dipper. The Little Dipper can be difficult to recognize because only three out of its seven stars are bright. The easiest way to identify Polaris is to first find the Big Dipper, which is made up of seven bright stars. The Big Dipper is part of constellation Ursa Major.

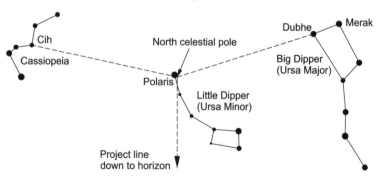

Draw an imaginary line from the last two stars of the dipper, Merak and Dubhe, and extend this line by five times to reach Polaris. If the Big Dipper is not in view, find Cassiopeia, which is made up of six bright stars and looks somewhat like a "W". From the center star, Cih, draw a line up and to the left to reach Polaris. To find due north, project an imaginary line straight down from Polaris to the horizon.

Finding due south

There is no bright star near the south celestial pole, so you have to visualize the south celestial pole as a fixed position between nearby stars. Find a distinct constellation called the Southern Cross (Crux), and two bright stars called Hadar and Rigil Kentaurus in the nearby constellation Centaurus. These last two stars are collectively known as The Pointers.

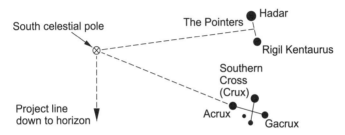

Draw an imaginary line between the two long-axis stars Gacrux and Acrux of the Southern Cross. Extend this line upward and a bit to the right by four times. This is the location of the south celestial pole. To confirm this position, connect a line between Hadar and Rigil Kentaurus. From the center of the connecting line, draw another line at right angle to the connecting line. Extend this line to where it intersects the line from the Southern Cross. To find due south, project an imaginary line straight down from the south celestial pole to the horizon.

5.4.2 Using stars to determine rough positions

With a star almanac, you may be able to use a bright star to determine your position without an angle-measuring device. Your derived position will be inexact and could easily be off by 100 km or more.

Latitude from zenith stars

Stars that pass directly above your location are called zenith stars. They are directly correlated to your latitude. After identifying a star that has passed directly overhead, just look up its declination in a star almanac or chart. Your latitude is the same as the star's declination. In almanacs, the declination is usually written as a negative number for latitudes south of the equator.

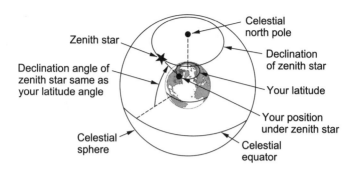

Example of using zenith star to find latitude

You observe the night sky for some time and notice a very bright star passing directly overhead. You recognize this star as being part of the Orion constellation. From a star chart, you identify the star as Rigel. A star almanac gives its declination as -08°14'. Your latitude is therefore 8°14'S. Round off this number to 8°S.

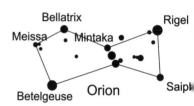

Longitude from stars at meridian transit

Your local celestial meridian is the projection of your longitude onto the celestial sphere. It's an imaginary line that runs through due north, zenith, and due south. Stars that are on your local celestial meridian at a particular moment are said to be at meridian transit.

Stars that are always above the horizon either reach their highest or lowest point above the horizon at meridian transit. Stars that are above the horizon half the time at your latitude always reach their highest point above the horizon at meridian transit. A star at meridian transit either has the same GHA (Greenwich hour angle) as your longitude, or a GHA that is 180° off from your longitude.

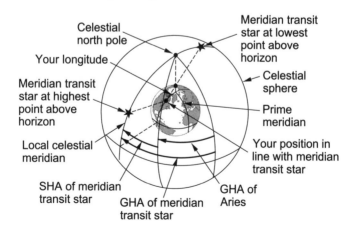

To take advantage of this phenomenon, you need a clock, a star chart, and an almanac. In practice, you will also need a compass or some other way to tell the direction of north or south. Set your clock to read universal time. Set your compass to 0° to view meridian transit stars to the north, or set your compass to 180° to view stars to the south. These bearings must be compensated for magnetic declination and point toward the geographic poles.

Aim your compass directly north or south and identify a bright star in that direction. For best accuracy, pick a star near the horizon. If there is no suitable star in either direction, wait for one to arrive. Write down the date and exact time when the meridian star was directly north or south. Identify the star using the star chart and then consult your almanac to obtain the star's GHA at that time and date. Your longitude is either the same as the star's GHA or off by 180°.

Example of using a star to find longitude

Aiming your compass straight north, you notice a bright star directly in line with the compass bearing. The date is October 28, 2007 and the time is 09:48:15 UT. You recognize the star as being part of the Cygnus constellation, and from the star chart identify the star as Deneb. Your almanac shows that Deneb has a SHA of 49°34.6'. At the time of observation, the GHA of Aries was 183°25.7'. The GHA of Deneb is thus 49°34.6' + 183°25.7' = 233°00.3'. Since this is greater than 180°, your longitude is east. Converting the hour angle to longitude gives 360°00.0' - 233°00.3' = 126°59.7'E. Round off this number to 127°E.

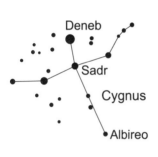

To figure out the direction of due north or due south without a compass, you could observe a star for some time and try to determine when it reaches its highest or lowest point above the horizon. This is very difficult without an angle-measuring device because the rate of change of height is minimal around meridian transit. A better method is to observe two stars that are located at the same SHA (sidereal hour angle) on the celestial sphere. These so-called transit pairs reach meridian transit at the same time. At that moment, one of the two stars will be directly above the other. An imaginary line drawn between the pair and extended down to the horizon will hit the horizon at right angles and the two stars will be aligned north-south.

Example of using transit pair to find longitude

A classic example of a transit pair is the stars Acrux and Gacrux in the Southern Cross constellation. These two stars aren't exactly on the same hour angle but close enough to determine your approximate longitude. Let's say you see the Acrux-Gacrux pair aligned more or less vertically to the horizon at 13:56:02 UT on December 17, 2003.

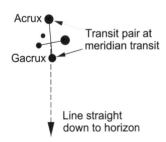

From an almanac, the SHA for Acrux is 173°18.2' and the GHA for Aries at that moment is 294°47.5'. The GHA for Acrux is 173°18.2' + 294°47.5' = 468°05.7' = 468°05.7' - 360° = 108°05.7'.

To confirm your result repeat the calculations for Gacrux. Its SHA is slightly different at 172°09.6'. The GHA for Gacrux is then 294°47.5' + 172°09.6' = 466°57.1' = 466°57.1' - 360° = 106°57.1'. Calculating the average GHA for the two stars gives (108°05.7' + 106°57.1')/2 = 215°02.8'/2 = 107°31.4'. Since this number is less than 180°, your longitude is west. Rounding off this number gives you an approximate longitude of 108°W.

You realize that this longitude is way off and by careful observation you notice why. The line down to the horizon points away from the south celestial pole. This means that the transit pair is in fact lower in the sky than the south celestial pole and must be at the lowest point in its orbit rather than the highest. The calculated longitude is therefore off by 180°. Your correct longitude is 108°W - 180° = -72°W = 72°E.

5.4.3 Stars as direction finders

At a given latitude, a particular star always rises at a certain fixed bearing, follows the same arc across the sky, and then sets at another fixed bearing. Bright stars that are low on the horizon can therefore be used to find directions, and are known as steering stars. To exploit this phenomenon, you need to create a star compass that shows the rising and setting bearings for all the important stars at your latitude (see example). This is best done with a celestial navigation calculator, but can also be done with a star almanac. Of particular interest are stars on the celestial equator, which rise exactly east and set exactly west from any latitude, and Polaris that always points north. Transit pairs at meridian transit can also act as steering stars because they point either north or south at that moment.

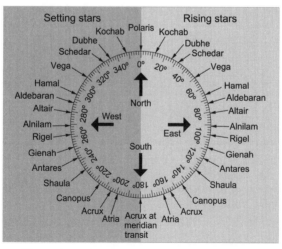

Example - star compass for latitude 10°N

All rising-setting stars approach or leave your horizon at an angle of 90° minus your latitude. For example, if you're at 30°S, the stars will rise or set at an angle of 60° relative to the horizon. Use this relationship to estimate the point on the horizon where a particular steering star has risen or will set. To determine the bearing of this point, consult your star compass for the star's rising or setting bearing. A steering star loses its usefulness as it moves too high in the sky. For continuous navigation throughout the night, use a series of steering stars that rise or set at different times.

5.5 Sextant navigation

The sextant is an angle-measuring device specifically designed for celestial navigation. It measures the vertical angle between a celestial body and the horizon. In sextant navigation, this angle is called the altitude of the celestial body. The process of measuring the angle is called taking a sight. To determine your position, take sights from at least two celestial bodies and record the exact times when these sights were taken. Perform several sets of calculations and then plot two or more lines of position on your chart. Your calculated position is the intersection between the lines of position.

Sextant navigation is not for people averse to complexity because of the elaborate procedure. The calculations are usually done with the help of tables with pre-calculated values or by using a celestial navigation calculator. This book only deals with the basic steps. Anyone contemplating navigating with a sextant should consult a book dedicated to the topic. Skip this section if your brain isn't working.

5.5.1 Underlying theory

Every celestial body is at zenith (directly overhead) at some location on Earth at a particular moment. The location directly below the celestial body is called the geographic position of the body. The geographic position moves as Earth rotates. In the case of the sun, moon, and planets, the geographic position also moves because of the body's and/or Earth's orbital motion. If you see a particular celestial body directly overhead at a certain time and know when and where this body is supposed to be at zenith, you will know your position. In practice, it's difficult to take advantage of this phenomenon because you are unlikely to be directly underneath an identifiable celestial body at a particular moment.

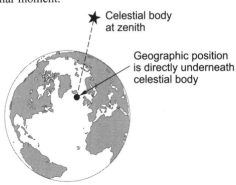

Celestial body at zenith

Geographic position is directly underneath celestial body

A more useful method is to observe a celestial body that is not at zenith. The geographic position of the body is then a certain distance and bearing from your location. Because of Earth's curvature, the celestial body appears lower on the horizon the further away you are from the body's geographic position. Most celestial bodies are so far away that their light rays are parallel anywhere on Earth. By measuring the angle between the celestial body and your horizon, you can calculate how far away you are from the geographic position. The smaller the angle, the further away you are. This angle is called the altitude of the celestial body and is what you measure when taking a sextant sight.

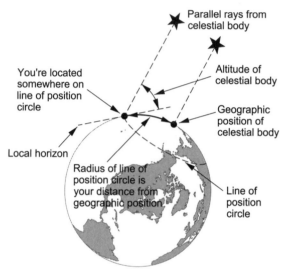

One sight establishes that you are located somewhere on a line of position circle that is centered on the geographic position of the celestial body, but does not tell you the direction to the geographic position. The "radius" of the circle is the distance along Earth's surface from your location to the geographic position. This radius is usually stated in angular units. To convert to distance units, use the formula: 1 minute of arc = 1 nautical mile = 1852 m.

Directly plotting a line of position circle on a chart is impractical in most cases because the geographic position is usually so far away that it is well beyond the boundaries of your chart. The usual procedure is to first select an assumed position somewhere on your chart near where you think you are. If you're using tables for your calculations, select an assumed position that will simplify subsequent calculations. With tables or a calculator, calculate the bearing and distance from your assumed position to the celestial body's geographic position. Use this information to plot a portion of an assumed line of position circle on your chart.

Because the geographic position is so far away, the portion of the circle that's on your chart is nearly straight, and is usually drawn as a straight line. After taking a sight, you can calculate the distance from your actual position to the geographic position. The difference in distance to the geographic position from your actual position versus from your assumed position is called the intercept.

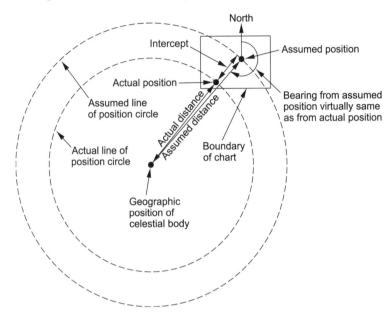

Because the geographic position is so far away, the bearing from your actual position to the geographic position is virtually the same as the bearing from your assumed position to the geographic position. On the chart, the actual line of position is a straight line parallel to the assumed line of position, but shifted by an amount equal to the intercept. The shift is either toward or away from the geographic position of the celestial body.

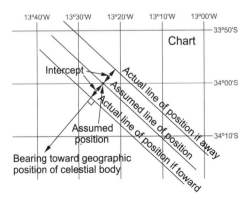

Taking sights from two celestial bodies establishes that you are simultaneously located on two line of position circles. This means that you must be on one of the intersections between the two circles. If you already know your approximate position, you should be able to eliminate one of the intersections. If not, take a third sight. Your position is the triple intersection between the three circles. Instead of taking sights of several celestial bodies, you can take several sights of the same celestial body at different times. Because the geographic position of the body moves, each sight gives you a new line of position circle.

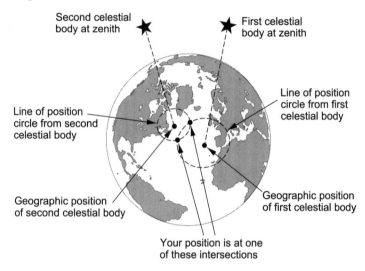

Taking a sight from a second celestial body and selecting a second assumed position enables you to plot a second line of position on your chart. Note that your second assumed position could be different from your first assumed position even if you haven't moved. The intersection between the two lines of position is your calculated position.

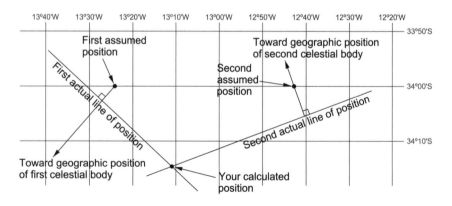

If you moved during the time interval between the two sights, you must shift the first line of position by your estimated movement since your first sight. Use dead reckoning (Section 8.3) to estimate this movement. Your calculated position is the intersection between the shifted first actual line of position and the second actual line of position.

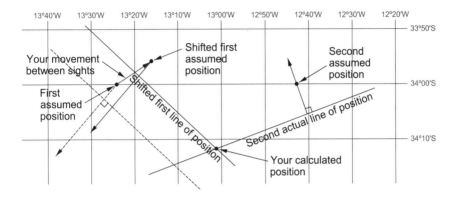

5.5.2 How the sextant works

The marine sextant consists of a triangular frame with a curved, graduated scale engraved on the bottom. A small telescope is attached horizontally on one side of the frame. Opposite the telescope is a fixed glass piece that is divided vertically into two sectors, one is transparent and the other reflective. Some sextants use one partially

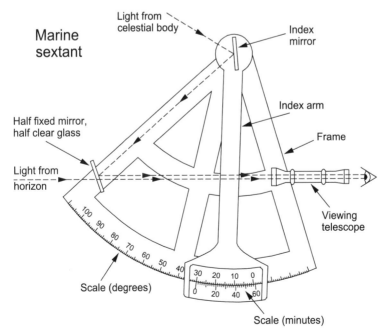

silvered mirror instead. An index arm is attached via a pivot joint to the top of the frame so that the lower part of the index arm can rotate across the graduated scale. An index mirror is attached to the index arm at the pivot joint.

This setup is designed so that the celestial body and the horizon can both be viewed at the same time through the telescope. When the index arm is turned to a certain angle, the celestial body will appear to be touching the horizon. At that moment, the scale will show the altitude of the celestial body, the vertical angle between the horizon and the body.

The marine sextant can only be used when you have an unobstructed view of the horizon. Other types of sextants that use artificial mercury or bubble horizons can be used anywhere but are not as accurate as the marine sextant.

5.5.3 Taking a sight

You need a clear view of both the horizon and the celestial body to measure the altitude of a celestial body with a marine sextant. With stars or planets you only have a small window of opportunity at dawn or dusk when it's light enough to see the horizon, but also dark enough to see the star or planet. A sight of the sun can be taken anytime it is visible. To avoid injuring your eyes, attach a dark sun filter before taking a sight of the sun.

With the scale set to zero, aim the telescope toward the celestial body. After finding the body, let the frame pendulum down without losing sight of the celestial body. To do this, you have to continually adjust the index arm. The horizon will come into view. Adjust the index arm so that the celestial body touches the horizon. Rock the sextant from side to side until the celestial body reaches its lowest point. This ensures that the sextant is held vertically. Fine-tune the index arm adjustment until the celestial body is exactly level with the horizon. With the sun or moon, make either the lower or upper limb touch the horizon.

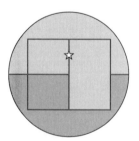 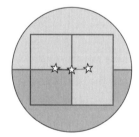 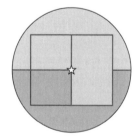

| Point telescope toward body and then bring body down toward horizon. | Rock sextant from side to side to ensure sextant is vertical. | With body on horizon and sextant vertical, read off the declination. |

Read off the altitude on the scale and write down the universal date and exact universal time (to the second) when the sight was taken.

5.5.4 Sextant calculations

There are two main methods to compute your position after taking sights of celestial bodies: (1) using an almanac together with sight reduction tables, or (2) using a celestial navigation calculator. The first method consists of a series of steps that involve looking up numbers in tables that are added or subtracted from each other. Your position is derived graphically from the intersection between lines of position on a chart.

Aside from being tedious, sextant calculations are riddled with jargon and acronyms, so it's easy to get confused. Develop a consistent routine to reduce the chance of error. The following procedure is an outline of how to compute a position fix the hard way by using an almanac and sight reduction tables. Each step is followed by an example. The best way to comprehend what is going on is to go through the calculations with an almanac and sight reduction tables at hand.

Take sextant sights

Check your almanac to see what celestial bodies it covers. Most almanacs have tables for the sun, moon, four planets, and 57 navigation stars. Take sights of at least two of these celestial bodies with your sextant. If only one body is visible, take several sights of that body at different times. For each sight, write down the sextant altitude (Hs), exact universal time (UT), and universal date (UD). If your clock is set to local time, convert your clock time to universal time and determine if the time conversion has changed the universal date. You also need to know the approximate locations where the sights were taken. This is usually accomplished by dead reckoning (Section 8.3).

On June 16, 2003 UD, you take a sight of the star Acamar at 22:15:46 UT. Reading off the sextant scale gives an altitude (Hs) of 61°42.8'. Your dead reckoning (DR) position at the time of the sight was 46°03.4'S, 127°19.7'E.

A few hours later when the universal date has changed to June 17, 2003, you take a sight of the lower limb of the sun at exactly 02:04.29 UT. The sextant gives an altitude (Hs) of 18°07.3'. You estimate that you've moved 38.9 nautical miles (nm) toward a bearing of 26° since your first sight. This gives you a dead reckoning (DR) position of 45°48.3'S, 128°13.9'E for the sun sight. Below is a summary of the results from this step:

Hs (Acamar) = 61°42.8', DR (Acamar) = 46°03.4'S, 127°19.7'E
Hs (Sun) = 18°07.3', DR (Sun) = 45°48.3'S, 128°13.9'E

Compensate for sight errors

The measured altitude of the celestial body isn't usually the exact angle between the horizon and the celestial body. You must compensate for: (1) the sextant's elevation above sea level at the time of observation, (2) any systematic index error in the sextant itself, (3) bending of light rays from the body by Earth's atmosphere, (4) whether the upper or lower limb of the sun or moon was used, and (5) parallax. The last factor applies only to moon sights, and is necessary because of the moon's proximity to Earth. After all the corrections are applied, the result is the body's observed altitude (Ho).

Let's say the sextant telescope was 3.1 m above sea level when the sights were taken. The "dip" column in the "altitude correction" tables gives a correction of -3.1' for a sextant height of 3.1 m. To determine the index error, read off the scale after taking a sextant sight of the horizon. Let's say the result is -2.6'. Compensating for the two corrections gives the apparent altitudes (Ha) of the bodies:

Ha (Acamar) = 61°42.8' - 2.6' - 3.1' = 61°37.1'
Ha (Sun) = 18°07.3' - 2.6' - 3.1' = 18°01.6'

The "altitude correction" tables also give the correction for atmospheric bending of light rays during different times of the year. For stars and planets the tables give a correction of -0.5' for Ha = 61°37.1. For the sun or moon, these tables give a combined correction for atmospheric bending and upper/lower limb compensation. This latter correction is necessary because the altitude of the center of the sun or moon is required for the calculations, while practical considerations dictate that a sight is always taken of the upper or lower limb of these two bodies. For the sun the tables give a combined lower limb/light bending correction of 13.4' for Ha = 18°01.6'. After the corrections have been applied, the result is the observed altitudes (Ho) of the bodies:

Ho (Acamar) = 61°37.1' - 0.5' = 61°36.6'
Ho (Sun) = 18°01.6' + 13.1' = 18°14.7'

Determine geographic position (GP) of body

The geographic position (GP) of a celestial body consists of its declination (latitude) and GHA (longitude) at the moment the sight was taken. The declination of the celestial bodies is given in the "daily" tables in the almanac. The "daily" tables also provide the GHA for the sun, moon, planets, and Aries meridian to the nearest hour. The "increment and corrections" table gives the GHA of all bodies to the nearest second. The SHA (sidereal hour angle) of the stars is written in one column of the "daily" tables.

For Acamar, the "daily" tables give a declination of 40°17.3'S, and a SHA of 315°24.6'. The "daily" tables also give a GHA for Aries of 234°45.3' at 22:00 UT on June 16, 2003. The Acamar sight was however taken at 22:15:46 UT so you must make up for the extra 15 minutes and 46 seconds past 22:00. The "increment and corrections" tables give 3°57.1' that must be the added to the GHA. The GHA for Acamar is therefore 315°24.6' + 234°45.3' + 3°57.1' = 554°07.0' = 554°07.0' - 360° = 194°07.0'.

The "daily" tables give a declination of 23°21.8'N for the sun. The GHA for the sun at 02:00 UT on June 17, 2003 is given as 209°49.3'. The sun sight was however taken at 02:04.29 UT so you need to compensate for the extra 4 minutes and 29 seconds past 02:00. The "increment and corrections" tables give an extra 1°07.3'. The GHA for the sun is therefore 209°49.3' + 1°07.3' = 210°56.6'. Below are the complete geographic positions (GP) of the bodies when the sights were taken:

GP (Acamar) = Dec 40°17.3'S, GHA 194°07.0'
GP (Sun) = Dec 23°21.8'N, GHA 210°56.6'

Select assumed position (AP) and determine local hour angle (LHA)

If the geographic position of a celestial body happens to be on your chart, you can immediately draw a line of position circle centered on the geographic position and with a radius equal to the observed altitude (Ho) of the body. The radius is converted from angle units to distance units using the conversion formula: 1 minute of arc (') = 1 nautical mile (nm). In most cases, the geographic positions are far outside the boundaries of your chart and you cannot directly draw a line of position circle on your chart. Instead, you must select an assumed position (AP) that is then readjusted based on the difference between the observed altitude (Ho) and the computed altitude (Hc) of the celestial body. Your AP must be selected as close as possible to, but generally not exactly, where you think you are.

To simplify subsequent calculations in the sight reduction tables, select an assumed position according to the following criteria: Select the assumed latitude to the nearest degree of your dead reckoning (DR) position. If the longitude is west, select the minutes of the assumed longitude to be equal to the minutes of the GHA of the body. If the longitude is east, select an assumed longitude so that its minutes plus the minutes of the GHA of the body add up to a whole degree (60').

The local hour angle (LHA) is the difference between your assumed longitude and the GHA of the celestial body. If your assumed longitude is east, add the assumed longitude to the GHA to get the LHA. If your assumed longitude is west, subtract the assumed longitude from the GHA to get the LHA.

Your DR position was 46°03.4'S, 127°19.7'E when the Acamar sight was taken. Select the assumed latitude to the nearest degree of the DR latitude, i.e. 46°S. Since your assumed longitude is east and the GHA of Acamar is 194°07.0', select an assumed longitude so that its minutes are 60' - 07.0' = 53.0'. The closest longitude to 127°19.7'E that matches this criterion is 126°53.0'E. Since the assumed longitude is east, add the longitude to the GHA to get the local hour angle (LHA) for Acamar: LHA = 194°07.0' + 126°53.0' = 321°.

Your DR position was 45°48.3'S, 128°13.9'E when the sun sight was taken. Select the assumed latitude to the nearest degree, i.e. 46°S. Since your assumed longitude is east and the GHA of the sun is 210°56.6', select an assumed longitude so that its minutes are 60' - 56.6' = 3.4'. The closest longitude to 128°13.9'E that matches this criterion is 128°03.4'E. Since the assumed longitude is east, add the longitude to the GHA to get the local hour angle (LHA) for the sun: LHA = 210°56.6' + 128°03.4' = 339°. Below is a summary of the results from this step:

AP (Acamar) = 46°S, 126°53.0'E

LHA (Acamar) = 321°

AP (Sun) = 46°S, 128°03.4'E

LHA (Sun) = 339°

Compute altitude (Hc) and azimuth (Zn) for assumed position (AP)

With the declination of the GP, the latitude of the AP, and the LHA as inputs, use the sight reduction tables to determine the computed altitude (Hc) and azimuth angle (Z) of the body. The computed altitude is the theoretical value of the altitude from the assumed position at the time of the sight. The azimuth angle is the smallest possible horizontal angle between the geographic position of the body and the nearest geographic pole as seen from your assumed position. Azimuth angles are either measured clockwise or counterclockwise. Before using an azimuth angle to plot a line of position, convert it to a true azimuth (Zn), which is always measured clockwise from the north pole like a true bearing.

For Acamar, the three input values into the sight reduction tables are: GP declination = 40°17.3'S, AP latitude = 46°S, and LHA = 321°. Find the page that is labeled LHA 321° and look in the section of the table that is labeled "latitude same name as declination". This latter directive is because the GP declination and the AP latitude are both south. For a declination to the nearest degree (40°), the table gives an initial computed altitude (Hc) of 61°09.3', an altitude difference (d) of +24.6', and an initial azimuth angle (Z) of 87.8°. Interpolating adjacent values in the table changes Z to 87.3°. A formula in the margin of the table states that "Zn = 180° - Z for southern latitudes and LHA greater than 180°". Therefore, Zn = 180° - 87.3° = 92.7°.

The altitude difference (d) is the difference between adjacent Hc values in the table. Find the "interpolation table" and use d (+24.6') and the minutes of the declination (17.3') as inputs. The table gives two correction factors, 5.8', and 1.3'. Since (d) is positive, add these two numbers to the initial Hc. The final Hc = 61°09.3' + 5.8' + 1.3' = 61°16.4'.

For the sun, the three input values are: GP declination = 23°21.8'N, AP latitude = 46°S, and LHA = 339°. Find the page that is labeled LHA 339°. Since the GP declination is north while the AP latitude is south, look in the section of the table that is labeled "latitude contrary name to declination". For a declination to the nearest degree (23°), the table gives an initial computed altitude (Hc) of 18°24.9', an altitude difference (d) of -57.9', and an azimuth angle (Z) of 159.7°. A visual interpolation changes Z slightly to 159.8°. A formula in the margin of the table states that "Zn = 180° - Z for southern latitudes and LHA greater than 180°". Therefore Zn = 180° -159.8° = 20.2°.

Find the "interpolation table" and use d (-57.9') and the minutes of the declination (21.8') as inputs. The table gives two correction factors, 18.2', and 2.8'. Since (d) is negative, subtract these two numbers from the initial Hc. The final Hc = 18°24.9' - 18.2' - 2.8' = 18°03.9'. Below is a summary of the results from this step:

Hc (Acamar) = 61°16.4', Zn (Acamar) = 92.7°.
Hc (Sun) = 18°03.9', Zn (Sun) = 20.2°.

Compare computed altitude (Hc) with observed altitude (Ho)

The difference between the computed altitude (Hc) and observed altitude (Ho) is the altitude intercept (a). The altitude intercept is the difference in radius between the line of position circle derived from the computed altitude (Hc) versus the one derived from the observed altitude (Ho). If Ho is bigger than Hc, move the line of position toward the geographic position of the body by the intercept distance. If Ho is smaller than Hc, move the line of position away from the body. The unit for the intercept, minutes of arc, is equivalent to nautical miles on Earth's surface.

For Acamar Hc = 61°16.4' and Ho = 61°36.6'. The intercept (a) = 61°36.6' - 61°16.4' = 20.2' = 20.2 nm. Since Ho is larger than Hc, move the line of position toward Acamar by 20.2 nm.

For the sun Hc = 18°03.9' and Ho = 18°14.7'. The intercept (a) = 18°14.7' - 18°03.9' = 10.8' = 10.8 nm. Since Ho is larger than Hc, move the line of position toward the sun by 10.8 nm. The intercept results are summarized below:

a (Acamar) = 20.2 nm toward GP of Acamar.

a (Sun) = 10.8 nm toward GP of sun.

Plot line of position (LOP)

Mark the assumed position (AP) of the first sight on your chart. Draw a line from the AP toward the celestial body's geographic position (GP) in the direction of the azimuth angle (Zn). Then, draw a line perpendicular to Zn and through the AP. This is your assumed line of position (LOP). Move the assumed LOP toward or away from the GP of the body by a distance equal to the altitude intercept (a) for that body. For best accuracy, use a plotting tool such as a protractor to draw the lines on the chart. Use an orienteering compass if no other tools are available.

Draw a LOP on the chart for each sight that you've taken. If all sights were taken from the same location, the intersection of the actual LOPs is your calculated position fix.

Mark the AP for Acamar (46°S, 126°53.0'E) on the chart. Draw a line from here in the direction of Zn (92.7°) and mark the end of the line with an arrow. Draw a line perpendicular to 92.7° and through the AP for Acamar. This is the assumed LOP for Acamar. Draw a second line parallel to the assumed LOP and shifted by a = 20.2 nm toward the GP of Acamar. This is the actual LOP for Acamar.

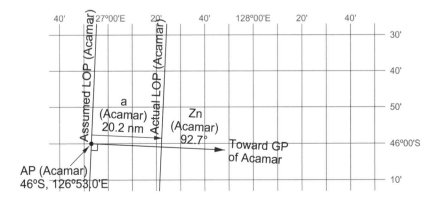

Mark the AP for the sun (46°S, 128°03.4'E) on the chart. Draw a line from here in the direction of Zn (20.2°) and mark the end of this line with an arrow. Draw a line perpendicular to 20.2° and through the AP for the sun. This is the assumed LOP for the sun. Draw a second line parallel to the assumed LOP and shifted by a = 10.8 nm toward the GP of the sun. This is the actual LOP for the sun.

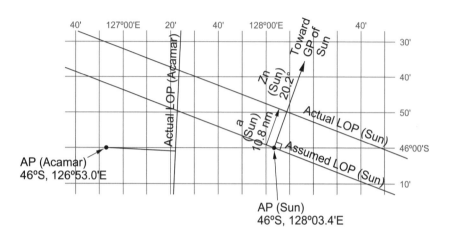

Shift line of position (LOP)

In many cases, particularly on the ocean, you will have taken sights from different locations. Before reading off your position fix, shift all the actual LOPs so that all the sights appear to have been taken from the location of the last sight. The dead reckoning (DR) positions that you used for earlier calculations will show you how to shift the LOPs.

On the chart, mark the DR positions of all the sights. Measure the distance and bearing from earlier DR positions to the DR position of the last sight. Then shift each earlier LOP by the measured distance and bearing. The intersection between the shifted LOPs and the LOP of your last sight is your calculated position fix.

Mark the DR position of Acamar (46°03.4'S, 127°19.7'E) and the DR position of the sun (45°48.3'S, 128°13.9'E) on the chart. Measure the distance and bearing from DR (Acamar) to DR (Sun). This yields a distance of 40.7 nm and a bearing of 68°. Shift the actual LOP of Acamar by 40.7 nm toward 68°. Your calculated position fix is the intersection between the shifted LOP of Acamar and the LOP of the sun. Use the latitude and longitude lines on the chart to read off the position fix, 45°52'S, 128°16'E.

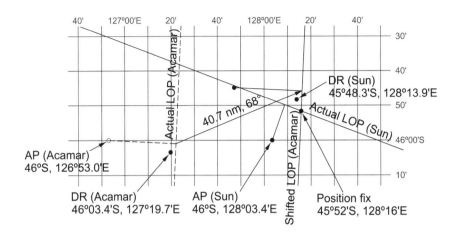

Using a calculator

By now you should have noticed that using an almanac and sight reduction tables to calculate your position requires a sharp mind and meticulous attention to detail. The task could prove challenging on a small water craft bouncing around in the middle of the ocean. A celestial navigation calculator will greatly simplify your calculations, assuming salt water doesn't destroy the unit. For each sight, plug in the sextant altitude (Hs), index error, sextant elevation above sea level, universal time (UT), universal date (UD), dead reckoning (DR) position, and select the appropriate celestial body. The calculator may ask if any LOPs have been shifted and will then automatically do all the calculations and spit out your position.

Chapter 6
Natural Navigation

Our ancestors were incredibly competent at using natural clues to navigate. Enhanced by thousands of years of experience, their techniques became ever more dependable. The same principles still apply today, although mastering ancient methods requires considerable tutoring and practice. Aside from being used as backups, natural navigation methods can help you travel faster and more efficiently when used in conjunction with modern navigation instruments. Keep in mind that many natural clues are specific to certain regions and may not work in your area. Use as many natural clues as possible to increase your odds of being correct. The best way to learn something about natural navigation is to make observations as you enter an area.

6.1 Effects of sunlight

The direction that a slope faces determines how much sunlight it receives. In the northern hemisphere, south-facing slopes generally receive more sunlight than north-facing slopes. The converse is true in the southern hemisphere where north-facing slopes receive more sunlight. The spring snow melts slower and glaciers are more likely to be present on slopes that face away from the sun. The vegetation may be denser or sparser on slopes that face the prevailing sun, depending on whether the added sunlight enhances growth or dries out the soil.

Certain plant and wildlife species are more plentiful on slopes that face the sun, while others that need moisture may favor slopes that face away from the sun. Berries usually ripen earlier and flowers grow more plentiful in the direction that receives the most sunlight. Conversely, certain types of mosses or lichens that require moisture may grow faster on the side of a tree or boulder that receives less sunlight. Many types of flowers face the prevailing sun. Some flowers track the sun during daylight hours, even when it is overcast. Trees can indicate the cardinal directions by the way they grow. The bark is often thicker on the side facing away from the sun. The branches on some species of tree grow bigger and more horizontal in the direction of the sun. One of the more reliable ways to tell the direction from a tree is to look at a stump. Tree rings are usually closer together in the direction of the prevailing sun.

Unfortunately, these clues don't always indicate a specific cardinal direction. Some species are less affected by sunlight than others. In many cases, the sunlight doesn't reach certain plants because they are shaded by terrain features or other nearby plants. For instance, trees growing along the perimeter of a forest normally receive more sunlight than trees in the middle of the forest, regardless of the direction of the prevailing sun. Other factors that influence growth such as soil, winds, or precipitation rates can mask the effect of sunlight. Analyze a large sample of plants in the same area and make sure you're completely familiar with the subject before drawing a definite conclusion.

6.2 Effects of wind

Differential heating of the atmosphere, together with the coriolis force of the spinning Earth, generates extensive bulk movement of air masses that creates enduring prevailing winds. The directions of the prevailing winds change with the seasons in some areas while in other regions they stay the same throughout the year. On land, the local topography often distorts the prevailing wind direction but surface winds nevertheless tend to blow from one preferred direction. From time to time, winds will blow from non-preferred directions.

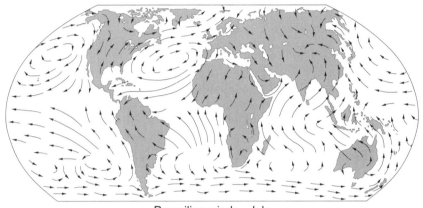

Prevailing winds - July

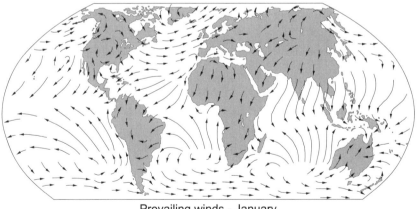

Prevailing winds - January

Knowing the direction of the prevailing wind in your area may help you determine the cardinal directions. If a high altitude wind is blowing, you can tell its direction by looking at the movement of high-level clouds. Surface winds often leave clues about their preferred direction even when they are not blowing. Persistent winds from a particular direction can modify the shape of trees by stunting the growth of foliage on the side facing the wind. In sand deserts, the wind molds the surface into sand dunes, and in similar fashion, the wind creates sastrugi (snow dunes) on snowfields. The most common type of sand dune or sastrugi is shaped like a ridge that runs parallel to the wind direction. This type of ridge has symmetrical sides. Another type looks like a horseshoe with its open end pointing away from the wind direction. A third type looks like sea waves with crests and troughs at right angles to the wind. Inhabitants of the arctic have used the shape of snow to travel in a straight line during whiteouts and desert nomads have used the shape of dunes to navigate during sand storms. The underlying principle is simple; just keep moving at a certain angle relative to the orientation of the sand dunes or sastrugi.

Snow cornices that form on mountain ridges give a clear hint of the preferred wind direction at that particular spot. They look like breaking sea waves that are frozen into position. Cornices are not necessarily useful for navigation because winds in mountainous terrain are often highly localized. The wind can spin around a mountain, creating cornices that point in several directions on the same mountain.

6.3 Landforms

In many parts of the world, mountain ranges, valleys, and rivers run parallel to each other. The easiest way to discover the landform pattern specific to your area is to look at a small-scale map or fly over the area. Take note of the cardinal directions of ranges and valleys and which way the rivers are flowing.

Repetitive landforms are a mixed blessing. By acting as guiding or catching features, the landforms can reveal your travel direction or tell you when you've reached a certain point. On the other hand, when all the landforms look alike, it may be difficult to tell one from another.

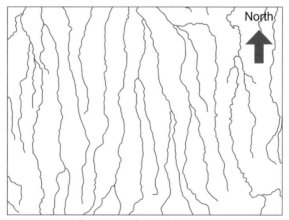

Example of parallel rivers

6.4 Ocean clues

The vast expanse of the open ocean with its lack of landmarks is an intimidating place for the untrained navigator. Yet, a lot of information can be gleaned by scrutinizing the surrounding sky and water. The unobstructed view on the ocean makes it an ideal place to use astronomical bodies to navigate, but there are other clues as well.

Ocean swells

Swells are different from locally generated waves. They are big waves that maintain their direction for a long time and are usually generated by prevailing winds. The heights of swells depend on the strength and duration of the generating wind, and the length of ocean over which the wind was blowing. The greater the distance from the generating wind, the longer the wavelength of the swells and the gentler the slope of the waves. Short wave lengths and steep slopes indicate that the generating wind is closer. Knowledge of general wind patterns gives you an indication of the general direction of the swells in your area.

Swells can persist for several days after the generating wind has stopped. This makes them well suited for maintaining your direction of travel on the open ocean. After pointing the bow of your vessel in the desired direction, determine the angle between the swells and your vessel and then maintain that angle to stay on course. A highly capable navigator can feel the direction of swells by the rocking motion of the vessel without looking outside. Close to shore, swell patterns are more complex and become difficult to predict.

Signs of land

There is often evidence of the direction and proximity to land long before it comes into view. Obvious signs include floating leaves, bark, branches, bushes, trees, or ice. Land can also literally be smelled. Clouds hovering in one location during an otherwise sunny day are an indication that there is land below. Local clouds commonly form over mountainous islands. The light of the sun or moon reflected off sandy beaches or smooth waters of sheltered lagoons can create a distinct glow above the land. Even during overcast days, light reflected from land can impart a different coloration to the clouds above.

Distorted wave patterns are often caused by waves reflecting back from land or squeezing between islands. Similarly, winds that suddenly change direction or turn gusty are an indication of nearby land. At night, the light from distant cities can be seen reflecting off clouds or smog.

Land-based seabirds are one of the most intriguing clues regarding the direction and distance to land. Some species of bird live on land but feed off the ocean. In typical fashion, these birds head out to sea in the morning to feed and return to land in the evening to rest. A navigator who spots a land-based bird in the morning may assume that land is in the direction that the bird is coming from, and in the evening simply follow the bird toward land. Potential changes to the birds' habits during nesting season must be taken into account. Instead of making one long trip per day, the birds may return to land several times to feed their young. Generally, the flight path of large groups of birds is a more reliable indicator of land than the movement of individual or small groups of birds.

Seamarks

The ocean isn't as uniform as many people think. Persistent warm or cold-water currents snake their way through water of different temperature or salinity, creating visible patterns for the observant navigator. You can estimate the water temperature by feeling it with your hand and determine its salinity by tasting the water. Nutrient rich water may look green compared to the bluish surrounding water. Light, shallow water stands out compared to dark deeper water. Certain types of water attract certain types of sea life. As a result, some locations on the ocean attract high concentrations of whales, sharks, jellyfish, sea birds, etc. It is a matter of knowing what type of water or sea life to expect at a particular location.

6.5 Making a compass

A magnetized nail, sewing needle, or wire can be made into a compass needle by placing it on a piece of paper or wood floating in a container of water. Make sure that the water container isn't made of ferromagnetic material. Plastic or aluminum are good candidates. Provided the setup isn't influenced by wind, the needle will quickly align itself along Earth's magnetic field lines.

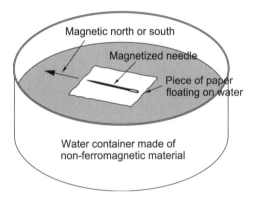

You will need additional information such as the direction of the sun to determine which end of the needle is pointing in the direction of the magnetic field lines (magnetic north). This setup is somewhat portable if you have a watertight lid on the container.

If the needle isn't magnetized, you may be able to magnetize it by repeatedly stroking the needle with a magnet. Always stroke with the same end of the magnet and toward the same end of the needle.

6.6 Using thermometer to determine elevation

The temperature of boiling water in an open pot depends on the ambient air pressure, which in turn is inversely proportional to your elevation. By boiling water in a pot and measuring the water temperature, you can calculate your approximate height above sea level. To do this, you need an accurate thermometer that can withstand being dipped in boiling water. At sea level, the boiling temperature of pure water is 100 °C. For every 300 m of elevation gain, the boiling temperature decreases by 1 °C. For a precise correlation, see Table 6.6.

Table 6.6
Correlation between elevation and boiling temperature of pure water

Temp.	Elevation	Temp.	Elevation
100.0 °C	0 m	85.0 °C	4500 m
98.3 °C	500 m	83.3 °C	5000 m
96.7 °C	1000 m	81.6 °C	5500 m
95.0 °C	1500 m	79.9 °C	6000 m
93.3 °C	2000 m	78.2 °C	6500 m
91.7 °C	2500 m	76.5 °C	7000 m
90.0 °C	3000 m	74.8 °C	7500 m
88.3 °C	3500 m	73.1 °C	8000 m
86.6 °C	4000 m	71.4 °C	8500 m

The accuracy of your reading will depend strongly on the accuracy of your thermometer and impurities in the water (don't use soup). Weather systems and other factors that influence altimeter readings will also affect your result.

Chapter 7
Emergency Communication

To call for outside assistance, you have a choice of many types of electronic communication devices. The technology is evolving so rapidly that it is difficult to keep pace with all the changes. There is also the danger of trying to use obsolete equipment that relies on infrastructure that no longer exists. You can, of course, resort to low-tech systems such as mirrors, flashlights, whistles, or flares to try to attract someone's attention.

7.1 Emergency transmitters

7.1.1 ELTs and EPIRBs

Battery-operated devices that can remotely locate an aircraft or ship in distress have been around for many years. In aviation, the device is called an emergency locator transmitter (ELT). In marine applications, it is known as an emergency position indicating radio beacon (EPIRB). The impact of a crash automatically activates an ELT, while an EPIRB is activated after the vessel is submerged. The buoyant EPIRB floats to the surface and starts transmitting. Both these devices can also be switched on manually. The distress signal is transmitted using one or more of the international search and rescue frequencies. A nearby aircraft or vessel that is equipped with a suitable receiver can pick up the distress signal and call for a rescue operation. The rescue craft uses a directional antenna to home in on the source of the distress signal.

Satellites can also pick up a distress signal and have the added advantage of surveying large areas and continual monitoring. After receiving a distress signal, the satellite relays the information to a ground station where the rough position of the signal source is calculated from the doppler shift of the distress signal. The doppler shift is the change in frequency of the distress signal that is caused by the relative motion between the emergency transmitter and the satellite. The accuracy of the position derived from the doppler shift is typically a few kilometers.

The most accurate emergency transmitters are used in conjunction with a GPS receiver. The GPS receiver is either a separate unit connected to the emergency transmitter or built into the emergency transmitter. The device transmits the position acquired from the GPS receiver to the satellites. A ground station that monitors the satellites relays the position to a local rescue organization. The accuracy of the transmitted position is equal to the accuracy of the GPS position fix.

7.1.2 Personal locator beacon (PLB)

A personal locator beacon (PLB) is a compact, lightweight emergency transmitter that operates in the same manner as an ELT or EPIRB, except that it can only be activated manually. A PLB can be highly effective at finding wilderness travelers in distress, especially if the PLB is used in conjunction with a GPS receiver.

Because of the potential for abuse and the great costs associated with false alarms, some jurisdictions dispense severe penalties for misuse and/or require that you register your PLB with the appropriate authorities. Some PLBs transmit a digitally encoded distress signal that, aside from relaying your position, also gives the rescuers other information such as the name of the registered owner of the PLB and what family members or friends to contact in case of an emergency. Most PLBs have enough battery power to transmit continually for up to a few days but this is reduced in cold temperatures. To avoid confusing rescuers, do not switch off a PLB once it has been switched on.

Other less sophisticated types of locator beacons are similar to transmitters used to track wildlife. They transmit a weak pulse at regular intervals and are always switched on. The batteries can last for a year or more. The transmitted signal is, however, not a distress signal and will not trigger a rescue unless you have prearranged for someone to start searching for you by a certain date. Typically, a rescue aircraft detects the transmitted signal and then homes in on the source using a directional antenna.

7.2 Two-way radios

A huge industry has been built around wireless communications and many types of two-way radios have been developed. Two-way radios use electromagnetic waves of certain frequencies to transmit and receive voice signals. Each frequency is associated with a particular radio channel. Most of the battery power of a radio is used when the unit transmits a signal. Much less power is used when only receiving a signal and even less when the radio is on standby. Carry spare batteries and shut off your radio when it is not in use.

Radios are averse to dirt and moisture, especially salt water, so make sure to protect your radio from the elements. Learn how to use your radio and carefully consider its limitations before heading into the wilderness. Make sure that your two-way radio has coverage for the area that you intend to travel. A common problem is the inability to receive or transmit a message. Just moving a few meters away can sometimes greatly improve or worsen your reception. Other times, you may have to move away from terrain features such as ridges that obstruct the signal or move to higher ground. Some radios are equipped with a switch that lets you adjust the transmitting power. Use the highest power setting if you cannot get any reception, but keep in mind that the higher power will drain the batteries faster.

Most aircraft and ships use geographic coordinates to navigate. Therefore, state your position in latitude and longitude when communicating directly with an aircraft or ship. On the other hand, local rescue organizations may prefer that you use grid numbers for your position. Be prepared to use both systems during an emergency.

Range

The range is the maximum distance that a two-way radio can transmit or receive an intelligible signal from a base station or another radio. The range increases with a more powerful transmitter, a bigger antenna, and a lack of obstructions. Unfortunately for the wilderness traveler, powerful transmitters are heavy, bulky, and draw a lot of battery power. In general, the lower the frequency of the radio wave, the greater the potential range. This is offset somewhat by the fact that low frequency radios require large antennas that are less efficient than small antennas. The range can increase considerably when atmospheric conditions allow the radio waves to refract (bend) along the curvature of Earth, or reflect (bounce) off the Earth's ionosphere or the ground before reaching the recipient.

Refraction occurs when radio waves pass between air masses of different densities. In the lower atmosphere, refraction normally increases the range by about 15 percent beyond the visible horizon for high frequency radio waves. Abrupt changes in air density can occur at certain elevations in the atmosphere due to temperature inversions or a sharp moisture gradient. Under these conditions, radio waves sometimes refract by the same amount as the curvature of the Earth, allowing communication over very long distances, especially if the transmitting and receiving radio antennas are in the same layer of air.

The upper atmosphere consists of several layers of ionized (charged) particles, most of which are created by sunlight knocking off electrons from the particles. Collectively, the ionized layers are known as the ionosphere whose thickness, height, and strength varies with the time of day and season. Radio waves that hit the ionosphere at certain angles are reflected back to the ground, increasing the potential range of the radio. The reflection angles depend on the frequency of the radio wave and the strength of the ionosphere. The radio waves may also reflect back and forth between the ionosphere and the ground, further increasing the range. At distances beyond the range of the direct signal but too close for the first reflected signal, there will be a zone where no transmission is possible. For frequencies higher than a certain threshold, all the radio waves will penetrate or be absorbed by ionosphere and no reflection will take place.

During nighttime, the ionized particles in the lower atmosphere recombine with electrons at a faster rate than they are separated and this part of the ionosphere weakens. This enables radio waves to reach and bounce off higher layers, which extends the range of radio waves at night.

7.2.1 FRS radios (walkie-talkies)

FRS (family radio service) radios, also known as walkie-talkies, are line-of-sight devices that are cheap, light, and easy to use. Most units offer a choice of several channels (frequencies). Just push a button to talk to anyone within range that has a similar device switched to the same channel. Release the button to listen. FRS radios are not subject to calling fees and normally no license is required.

The units use the same frequency to transmit and receive, so you cannot talk and listen at the same time. As the name suggests, FRS radios are mainly used to communicate between members of a group. The low-power transmitters in FRS radios provide a maximum range of only 1 to 3 km, making the units unsuitable to call for distant outside help. Some units can tune into broadcast radio stations, a useful feature for getting weather forecasts

A serious drawback is the lack of a world standard for allowable radio frequencies. An FRS radio purchased in one country that allows a certain set of FRS frequencies may be illegal in another country that allows a different set of frequencies. Using an FRS radio in the wrong country could interfere with communications by that country's police, military, etc., and may be subject to harsh penalties. On the other hand, if you are deep in the wilderness and away from other people, your FRS radio signal is unlikely to interfere with anyone outside your group.

7.2.2 VHF/UHF radios

VHF (very high frequency) or UHF (ultra high frequency) radios are similar to FRS radios but are much more powerful. They are used by pilots, sailors, police, fire fighters, rescue teams, and by many other professionals and amateurs. In certain areas, they can also receive weather forecasts. The range is normally line of sight but can be extended considerably by repeater stations that retransmit the radio signals to other two-way radios or into telephone networks.

A huge bureaucracy has been created governing the use of VHF/UHF radios. Some channels are off limits to the public and some jurisdictions require that you get an operator license and/or register your radio. There are also regulations on what you can talk about on certain channels. Of particular interest to wilderness travelers, are the emergency channels that are specifically used to call for a rescue. For instance, if you want a VHF/UHF radio for ocean kayaking, make sure that your radio can access the marine emergency channel for the area that you intend to travel. Before purchasing or renting a VHF/UHF radio, find out what channels are available on the radio and who, if anyone, monitors these channels for your area of travel.

Emergency call procedure

During an emergency, you must decide whether to do a mayday or pan-pan call. Mayday calls are reserved for situations where there is immediate risk to life. For example, you are seriously injured, about to succumb to hypothermia, or clinging to an overturned kayak. Pan-pan calls indicate that you need help but are not in immediate danger. For example, you have a non-life threatening injury that prevents you from traveling, but have enough supplies to survive for several days.

1. Prepare ahead of time what you are going to say, then switch on your VHF or UHF radio. Select the emergency channel if there is one for your area. To avoid overriding other calls, wait for a gap in the transmission before calling.

2. Press the transmit button, say "mayday, mayday, mayday" or "pan-pan, pan-pan, pan-pan", and briefly state the nature of your emergency and your position (if known). Speak slowly and clearly and end the sentence with "over."

3. Release the transmit button and wait for a reply. If you don't get a response after about a minute, repeat the entire broadcast. Continue calling periodically, even if you get no answer. It's possible that your radio is transmitting but not receiving.

4. If you still cannot get a response, try calling on another channel and, if possible, move to a location with better reception. Keep in mind that the reception may be better at certain times of day or night.

7.2.3 HF radios

HF (high frequency) radios are capable of long distance communication, but the quality of the reception is governed by atmospheric conditions and the time of day. Although the range of the direct signal is limited to your line of sight, reflected signals can extend the range to several hundred kilometers. The unit can be both heavy and bulky. Two long wire antennas must be strung out before the radio can be used. For best reception, lay out the antennas as high as possible and at right angles to the radio that you are trying to reach. An HF radio may be equipped with several sets of antennas of different lengths. Each antenna set is designed to be used with a specific radio channel, so you must change the antennas when you switch channels. In general, the lower the channel frequency, the longer the corresponding antenna. At night, your HF radio may be subject to interference from distant radio stations. The main limitation of HF radios is the weight of the radio and the elaborate antenna setup. The emergency call procedure is the same as for VHF or UHF radios.

7.2.4 Cellular phones

Cellular phones are widely available and mainly used for mindless chatter, but have occasionally saved lives. Unlike FRS, VHF, UHF, or HF radios, cellular phones cannot communicate directly with each other. The call must first go through a base station transceiver that then relays the signal through a telephone network to other phones.

Both the phone and the base station use low-power transmitters, so the direct range of the signal is limited to only a few kilometers. This isn't a problem around most urban areas where extensive grids of base stations have been built. Your cellular phone simply switches from one base station to the next as you travel. The short range is deliberate and allows the reuse of the same frequency by non-adjacent base stations so that many cellular phones can be used at the same time without interference. A cellular phone is easy to use although the underlying technology is complicated. The signal is digitally compressed and coded and can simultaneously be sent over several channels, some of which may be shared with other callers. The system automatically handles billing of phone calls.

For your cellular phone to work, you must be within range of a base station that belongs to, or is affiliated with, your service provider. During an emergency, you may not be able to complete a call despite being within range of a base station. Before heading out into the wilderness, make sure that the phone's batteries are fully charged. Protect your phone from moisture and remember that your phone becomes useless as you move away from the base station grids.

7.2.5 Satellite phones

Satellite phones generally have very broad coverage but not necessarily global. Depending on your service provider, your satellite phone uses either a few geostationary satellites that hover over the same point above Earth's equator, or a large number of satellites in much lower orbits. The signal from your phone travels directly to one or more of the satellites where it is relayed to a ground station and into the telephone network. If your phone uses geostationary satellites, you must point the phone's antenna directly toward one of the satellites to get reception. This type of phone usually has a small, built-in compass and a booklet telling you where to aim the phone. Because geostationary satellites are located high (36 000 km) above Earth, the signal travels a considerable distance before reaching your recipient and vice-versa, and there is a noticeable time delay during conversations. If your phone uses low-orbit satellites, you normally only need to point your phone's antenna upward to lock onto one of the satellites and there is no noticeable time delay during conversations.

Both the transmitted and received signals are low-power and the phone probably won't work under heavy tree cover or in deep canyons. You need an unimpeded view of the sky for clear reception and to avoid being cut off during a conversation. Some satellite phones are able to use the cellular network. This type of phone will function just like a cellular phone when it's within range of a cellular base station. When you move beyond the cellular range, the phone automatically switches to direct communication with satellites.

7.2.6 Miscellaneous wireless devices

New types of wireless communications devices are being introduced at an unrelenting pace. The wireless signals could be transmitted via the cellular network or directly via satellites, or both. Any new type of wireless device would be subject to the same type of limitations that afflict cellular and satellite phones.

With digital technology, wireless devices can be designed to transmit and receive just about any kind of information. For example, with the proper equipment you could e-mail someone for help or activate someone's pager. Another possibility would be to use your digital camera to take pictures of your surroundings and then send the pictures over your wireless device to a rescue team. The rescuers could analyze the terrain in your pictures and then advise you how to proceed. The possibilities are as limitless as the ways things can go wrong.

7.3 Signaling systems

Signaling systems serve two main purposes: requesting assistance and guiding rescuers toward your location. Anything that attracts attention to your situation such as flashlights, whistles, mirrors, flares, or bright clothing can be used for signaling. For maximum effect, make sure your signal looks or sounds as different as possible from your surroundings. For example, if you're on snow use something dark to attract attention, or conversely, don't use an acoustic device that sounds like a bird if you're in a bird sanctuary. Do not depend on just one signaling system. Be prepared to use every conceivable method that you can think of.

One of your most important decisions is choosing when to deploy consumables such as flares. You are faced with the conflicting demands of taking advantage of an important opportunity versus conserving a valuable resource. Your decision should be based on the likelihood of anyone detecting your signal, recognizing it as a call for help, and then initiating a rescue. Set up your signaling systems ahead of time so that you can activate them at a moments notice when the opportunity arises. Rescuers may respond to your signals with their own signals. If that happens, repeat your distress signal to help rescuers home in on your location.

7.3.1 Flares

Two main types of emergency flares exist: ground flares and aerial flares. Ground flares either spray burning material or colored smoke out of one end of the flare. Colored-smoke flares are meant to be used during the day, while burning material flares work best at night. Aerial flares use a small rocket to shoot up a charge into the air. When the rocket fuel is spent, the charge ignites and starts glowing. A small parachute deploys and the glowing charge slowly descends to the ground. Aerial flares are either handheld or launched from specially designed flare guns. Most types of aerial flares are intended for marine use only because of the danger of starting a forest fire when the flare lands on the ground.

For distress purposes, your flares should emit either red or orange light or smoke, but don't hesitate to use other colored flares if they are available. Flares are potentially dangerous devices that require proper operation and storage. Read the instructions before firing one off and make sure the flare is pointed in the correct direction. Moisture or age can cause flares to misfire.

7.3.2 Mirrors

In bright sunlight, a good mirror reflects an enormous amount of light that can be seen from far away. A mirror compass can be used for this purpose. Other reflective surfaces such as sunglasses, watch faces, or shiny metal surfaces do not reflect nearly the same amount of light as a glass mirror. The difficult part is aiming the sunlight toward your target. Specially designed signaling mirrors are equipped with a sighting apparatus that makes aiming the mirror much easier.

To aim an unsighted reflecting surface, close one eye and point the tip of your thumb toward your intended target. Hold the reflecting surface as close to your open eye as possible and orient the reflecting surface so that the reflected sunlight hits the tip of your thumb. This will direct the reflected sunlight toward your target. Wiggle the reflecting surface to direct a flickering signal at your target.

7.3.3 Light signals

You can use a flashlight or any other battery operated light source to send distress signals at night and even during the day. The standard emergency procedure is to use the light source to send an SOS signal. This is done in Morse code with a sequence of three short flashes, followed by three long flashes, and then three more short flashes. Aim your light toward a logical target and repeat the signal sequence as many times as necessary.

In general, strobe lights do not have the same range as flashlights, although a rapidly flashing light will certainly draw the attention of anyone who sees it. One advantage is that they can be left unattended for extended periods. A camera flash will also work as a signaling device. Another tool is a specially designed signal laser. The low dispersal of the laser beam means that the light carries over long distances. Signaling lasers must be oriented a certain way because the beam is typically projected as a line of light rather than a point. Because of the narrow beam, aim the laser directly at your target to attract attention. If your laser lacks a sighting apparatus, use the same technique as with a mirror to direct the laser beam at the target. Once the beam is aimed, move it very slowly back and forth across your target.

7.3.4 Fires

Fires can be an effective signaling method. The universal distress signal is three fires positioned 10 - 15 m apart and arranged in a triangle. Setting up signal fires requires a lot of preparation, especially if you are in an area that lacks much combustible material.

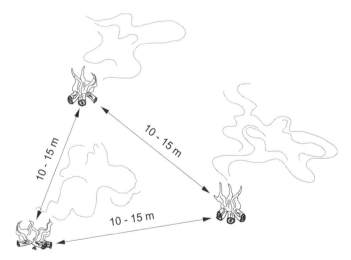

To avoid maintaining three continually burning fires, only light one of your three "fires" and set the others up for quick ignition. Prepare the unlit "fires" by gathering plenty of dry kindling into a pile and then adding some green vegetation to the top of the kindling. The green vegetation will ensure that the fire produces enough smoke to be visible from the air. If a low flying aircraft approaches, quickly ignite all your "fires".

7.3.5 Acoustic devices

The sound of an acoustic device such as a whistle or an air horn carries much further in the wilderness than shouting. Acoustic devices are intended to catch the attention of anyone within audible range. The universal distress signal is the SOS sequence with three short blasts, followed by three long blasts, and three more short blasts repeated at regular intervals. A series of three blasts repeated over and over is also considered a distress signal. A whistle is a lightweight and durable device that should be carried by every wilderness traveler. Rain, snow, and heavy vegetation will reduce the acoustic range. Wind normally decreases the range but can in some instances increase the down-wind range.

7.3.6 International ground signals

Aircrews that are trained in search and rescue techniques should understand the international ground signals. The aircraft can acknowledge your message by tipping its wings or flashing a green light. An aircraft that flashes a red light or flies in a clockwise circle may mean that your message is not understood. Some of your signals will be in response to questions from the aircraft. The aircrew can for example drop you a message from the aircraft or talk to you via a megaphone.

Ground symbols

Ground symbols can be stomped into the snow, drawn in the ground, written with a pattern of rocks, etc. Make the characters as large as possible so that they are clearly visible from the air. If you haven't memorized any of these ground symbols, write out "RESCUE" or "SOS" instead.

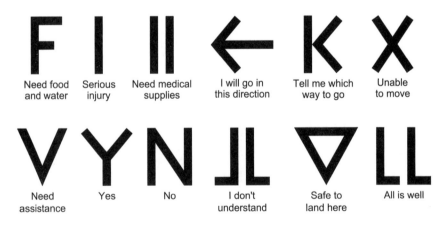

F	I	II	←	K	X
Need food and water	Serious injury	Need medical supplies	I will go in this direction	Tell me which way to go	Unable to move

V	Y	N	⅃	▽	LL
Need assistance	Yes	No	I don't understand	Safe to land here	All is well

Body signals

Body signals have similar meanings as ground symbols except that you can respond instantly to any questions from the aircrew. For greatest effect, wear clothing that contrasts with the color of your background. For a signal that requires you to move your arms, hold a bright cloth in your moving hand and exaggerate the movement.

Pick us up   Yes   No   Have radio   All is well

Land in this direction   Do NOT attempt to land here   Need medical assistance   Use drop message   Can proceed shortly

Chapter 8
Practical Navigation

How you navigate is largely dictated by the availability of landmarks. If prominent landmarks are visible, you should be able to navigate with only a map, or in some cases, just your memory as a guide. When no landmarks are visible, you must complement your map with a compass and use techniques such as dead reckoning to estimate your position. For land navigation, an altimeter will often enhance your ability to establish your location. For long trips through featureless terrain, a position-finding device such as a GPS receiver or sextant is required.

8.1 Terrain association – map only

Navigating by terrain association requires prominent landmarks, a certain amount of visibility, and a map if the terrain is unfamiliar. Terrain association is based on building a mental image of the terrain. The surrounding landmarks and linear features guide your movement. Linear features are long, thin features that can be straight or curved. They include valley bottoms, canyons, rivers, coastlines, ridges, power lines, and roads.

You can usually find your way without too much effort with terrain association, provided a significant portion of the terrain is visible. It is a natural way of navigating; it's how we subconsciously do it in everyday life. If you plan to travel through an unfamiliar area, try building an initial mental image of the area ahead of time by studying maps and pictures. As you travel through the new area, your mental image is continually modified by what you see in the real world. The key to success is your ability to recognize certain critical features on both the map and in the real world.

Here are a few important considerations:

- Orient the map. It's much easier to compare the map with the real world when the map is oriented. Use prominent landmarks or the sun to orient your map.

- To identify features, look at the shape and steepness of slopes, the relative heights and directions between features, and the directions and relative elevations between you and the features. Look for any other clues such as vegetation zones or the direction of running water.

- Do mental triangulations off visible landmarks to estimate your position on the map.

- Keep track of which direction you're heading and estimate the distance you've traveled since your last known position. To keep yourself moving in the correct direction, adjust your travel direction relative to distant landmarks or follow linear features that are parallel to your travel direction. Don't forget to look at the landmarks behind you.

- Select catching features to alert you when to change direction or if you've gone too far. Catching features are linear features that cross your line of travel or landmarks whose nearby presence you're unlikely to miss.

Navigational errors are easily spotted with terrain association. If you encounter something in the real world that contradicts what you expected from the map, you immediately know that you are not were you though you were. There is, of course, the possibility that your map is incorrect. Terrain association requires lots of practice to master. It also lacks the precision needed for finding exact locations and is difficult to use when the visibility is poor.

Example of terrain association

With the map below as your only navigation tool, you intend to hike from (A) to a campsite by a lake at (D).

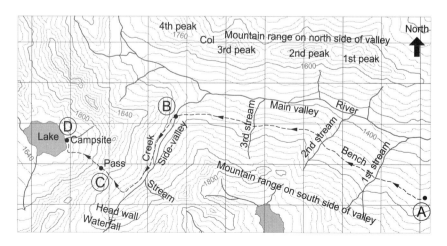

The first part of your journey follows a bench that runs along the south side of an east-west tending valley. A bench is a flat section on a slope. A mountain range runs along each side of the valley. A river flows along the bottom of the valley with several small streams tumbling down into the river from the flanks of the mountains. Knowing which direction to travel on this part of the route is easy. Just travel parallel to the river. If you drift too far to the right or left, you will run into steeper ground.

To figure out of how far you've traveled along the bench, pay attention to the surrounding features. Counting the number of streams that you cross may seem like an obvious method but all streams aren't necessarily marked on your map. A more dependable method is to keep track of the peaks that rise along the sides of the valley. The tops of the peaks on the south side of the valley are probably hidden from view because of your location on the same side of the valley. You are more likely to have an unobstructed view of the peaks on the opposite, north side of the valley.

Your first catching feature is the creek that drains the first major side-valley that you encounter to the south. This creek is bigger than the other side-streams because it drains a larger area. The side-valley is also much wider than the gullies that drain the other streams and you may be able spot the headwall and waterfall to the south. To confirm that you've reached the correct creek, look at the peaks on the north side of the main valley. You should be opposite from the col that separates the 3rd peak from the 4th peak.

After crossing the creek at (B), head up the side-valley. The navigation here is easy. Just follow the creek upstream. The next navigation challenge is finding the pass at (C). Pay close attention to the peaks on both sides of the valley. There is no obvious catching feature that tells you where to start your upward climb toward the pass. If you reach the headwall with the waterfall, you have gone too far. Assuming that each grid square represents 1 km x 1 km, the map shows that you must head upward toward the pass about 1 km before reaching the headwall. This location is about halfway between the headwall and a major stream that runs down the east side of the side-valley.

If you start climbing at the correct location, the terrain will funnel you toward the pass (C). After reaching the pass, head downhill toward the center of the lake. The lake is at the bottom of a basin and any streams that you encounter in this area will run into the lake. Keep this in mind in case the fog rolls in and you suddenly lose sight of the lake. In addition, heading down the fall line (steepest slope direction) will bring you directly to the lake. Turn right at the lake and follow the shoreline. The campsite should be near the first major stream flowing into the lake (D). Do mental triangulations off the peaks that surround the basin to confirm your location.

8.2 Conventional map and compass navigation

Prominent landmarks and linear features are often blocked from view by terrain, foliage, or fog. Other lesser features that are visible can be difficult to identify if they are too plentiful, or too small to show up on your map. Under these circumstances, it can be difficult to travel in the correct direction without a compass.

A compass allows you to travel in the correct direction even when you cannot see anything except your immediate surroundings. It also allows you to pinpoint your position by triangulation whenever landmarks are visible. The following steps describe conventional map and compass navigation. If necessary, review Chapter 2 for detailed information on how to use a compass.

1. If your compass is equipped with an adjustable magnetic declination mechanism, adjust the declination so that it conforms to grid north. If not, add or subtract the declination after taking each map or field bearing.

2. If you don't already know where you are on the map, use terrain association or compass triangulation to find your position. Do this before it gets dark or the fog rolls in.

3. Plot a proposed route on the map from your current position to your desired destination. If necessary, break up the route into a series of straight-line segments. The junctions between segments are called waypoints, and are intermediate targets that you will reach during your journey.

4. Take a bearing off the map, from your current position to the next waypoint along your route. If the waypoint is located along a catching feature, add or subtract a deliberate offset to your compass bearing. The offset bearing will guide you toward the catching feature rather than directly toward the waypoint. The catching feature is usually much easier to find than the waypoint. Don't use an offset bearing if there is no catching feature.

5. Follow the compass bearing toward the catching feature or waypoint. Use steering marks to avoid constantly looking at your compass. The further you travel along the bearing, the more likely you are to drift off course, so take the opportunity to pinpoint your position by triangulation or terrain association whenever suitable landmarks appear.

6. Once you reach the catching feature, the direction of the offset bearing will govern whether you go right or left along the catching feature to reach the waypoint. If you've been following a non-offset bearing, you will hopefully stumble right onto the waypoint.

7. Once you reach the first waypoint, repeat the above steps for subsequent waypoints along your route.

Example of map and compass navigation

You are somewhere along the shoreline of a lake (A) and intend to hike over a mountain range to the outlet of a second lake (F). After analyzing your map, you decide to travel to your destination via two passes, (C) and (D), and a creek fork (E). To shorten your first segment, you will triangulate your position at the first creek crossing (B).

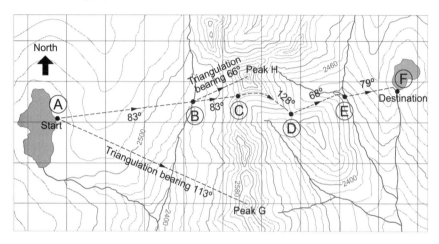

Adjust the declination on your compass so that it conforms to grid north. To triangulate your initial position, take a field bearing off Peak G, a convenient landmark that is visible from the lake. The result is a bearing of 113° whose line of position intersects the lakeshore at (A), your current position. Taking a bearing off the map from (A) to (C) gives a bearing of 83°. Follow this bearing to the creek. From the creek bed, a field bearing off Peak H gives 66°. The line of position from this bearing intersects the creek at (B), which becomes your triangulated position.

A map bearing from (B) to (C) gives 83°, confirming that you've maintained the correct course from (A). Continue along this bearing. As you climb higher, the terrain will funnel you toward the first pass at (C). After reaching the pass, maintain a constant elevation as your contour along the south slopes of Peak H to its southeast ridge. Follow the ridge downward along a bearing of 128° to the pass at (D).

From the pass at (D), take a map bearing to the creek fork (E). The result is 73°. Subtracting 5° gives an offset bearing of 68°. Follow the offset bearing to the creek. Take a right at the creek and follow it downstream to the fork.

The last bearing (84°) is toward your final destination (F). Here you have a choice of two catching features, the lake, or the creek that flows out of it. The lake is a better choice because the creek could potentially be confused with a stream not marked on your map. Subtract 5° for an offset bearing of 79° and follow this bearing to the lake. Take a right at the lake and follow the lakeshore to your destination at the outlet (F).

8.3 Dead reckoning – no landmarks

The word "dead" in dead reckoning may have been derived from its original meaning "deduced". In this book, dead reckoning is defined as navigating with just a map (or chart) and a compass when no landmarks are visible. The underlying assumption is that if you start from a known position, and are diligent about recording how far and in what direction you've traveled, you can figure out where you are. The main application of dead reckoning is for travel across large open spaces such as deserts, tundra, polar plateaus, or oceans, often in conjunction with celestial navigation. Dead reckoning is also used for travel through ordinary terrain during periods of reduced visibility or through thick undergrowth.

Although it has been used successfully by highly competent navigators, dead reckoning is inherently unreliable because it is difficult to maintain a straight course and judge how far you've traveled. At sea, you must compensate for the drift caused by winds and currents. The further you travel, the more the errors accumulate, particularly if you're forced to veer off a straight-line course. All it takes is one mistake and you're lost. Navigating by dead reckoning involves three interrelated activities: (1) keeping track of bearings, (2) keeping track of distance, and (3) detouring around obstacles.

8.3.1 Keeping track of bearings

Keeping track of bearings is practical only if you travel along straight-line segments. Any curved paths will greatly complicate your task and should be avoided. Unless obstacles block your route, stick to rigid straight-line segments by following a specific compass bearing to the end of each segment. Diligently record the bearings for all the segments that you have completed.

8.3.2 Keeping track of distance

Figuring out the distance traveled along each segment is the most difficult part of dead reckoning. Your mode of travel will largely dictate what distance measuring techniques you can use.

- If you're hiking, multiply your average stride length by the number of steps that you've taken. To calculate your average stride length, count how many steps it takes you to complete a known distance, then divide the known distance by the number of steps. While traveling, move pebbles or matchsticks from one pocket to another to keep track of your step-count. For example, move one pebble from one pocket to the other for every 100 steps. Electronic step counters are available that strap to your hip and count your steps by sensing the movement of your hip. The unit displays your travel distance based on your stride length. Read the instruction manual for procedures on how to calibrate the step counter so that it conforms to your stride. Keep in mind that different types of terrain will substantially alter your stride length.

- If you're traveling roped up on snow, use the rope length to measure the distance. The first person on the rope draws a line in the snow. When the last person on the rope reaches this line, he or she signals to the first person to draw another line in the snow. As this process is repeated, the last person keeps track of the number of lines. Multiply the number of lines by the length of rope between the first and last person to calculate the distance.

- An odometer wheel can be towed along or attached to a sled or cart. As you travel the odometer counts the number of revolutions of the wheel. To calculate the distance, measure the circumference of the wheel and then multiply the circumference by the number of revolutions. This method has been used successfully on polar sledding expeditions.

- If you know your average travel speed, you can calculate your distance by keeping track of your travel time. On land, judge your speed from previous travel through similar types of terrain. On the water, measure the time it takes for the length of your boat to travel past a wave top or piece of driftwood. Divide the length of your boat by the time, to obtain the speed of your boat. To compensate for drift caused by wind and waves, look at the wake of your boat. Your travel direction is in line with the wake, not the direction where the bow is pointing. Compensating for currents is very difficult on the open ocean but relatively easy on rivers. Once you've estimated your speed, multiply your speed by your travel time to obtain the distance.

8.3.3 Detouring around obstacles

Circumventing obstacles while moving along a dead reckoning segment must be done without losing your distance measurement tally. Follow detour segments that are either perpendicular or parallel to your original travel direction. Instead of readjusting your compass bearing, travel at right angles to the travel direction arrows on your compass while following a perpendicular detour segment.

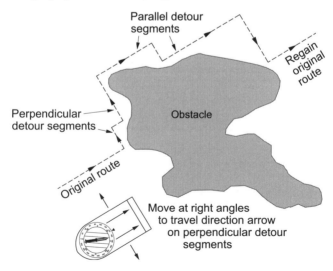

You must keep track of two separate distances during the detour. Add the distances of the parallel detour segments to your original route tally. Either add or subtract the distances of the perpendicular detour segments, depending on whether you're moving away or toward your original route. The total perpendicular distance of the detour segments will cancel out when you regain your original route on the other side of the obstacle.

You can avoid the perpendicular count if there is a steering mark in line with your original route on either side of the obstacle. Just keep track of the distance along the parallel detour segments during the detour. You will regain the original route when you reach the steering mark on the far side of the obstacle. If the steering mark is on the near side of the obstacle, use a back bearing to regain your route. If the obstacle is big enough to show up on your map, pinpoint your position by terrain association and then use the obstacle as a starting point for a new dead reckoning segment.

8.3.4 How to navigate with dead reckoning

There are two main ways to use dead reckoning: (1) plotting your route ahead of time on the map and then following that route in the real world, or (2) using dead reckoning to estimate your position after you have already traveled.

Following a predetermined dead reckoning route

1. Determine the location of your starting point on the map by using terrain association or triangulation. Dead reckoning will not work without a known starting point.

2. Plot your route as a series of straight-line segments that follow your desired line of travel. Keep your route as simple as possible by using the minimum number of segments. Label as waypoints the connection points between the segments.

3. Take compass bearings off the map between all adjacent waypoints along your route. Write down the bearings and note whether the bearings are relative to true north, grid north, or magnetic north.

4. Measure the distance of each segment with a graduated ruler. Use the map scale to calculate the real world distance of each segment. Write down the real world distances.

5. Now you're ready to navigate. Set your compass to the bearing between the first two waypoints. If necessary, readjust the bearing to take into account the magnetic declination. Follow the compass bearing while keeping track of the distance traveled along the segment. To stay on course without constantly looking at your compass, use steering marks or natural clues such as the direction of your shadow. If you're on a large body of water, adjust your boat's heading to compensate for winds and currents. This will affect your speed toward the waypoint.

6. Once your distance tally shows that you've reached the first waypoint, repeat the procedure for subsequent segments until you reach your destination. If you inadvertently travel past a waypoint, you can re-plot your course rather than backtrack to the missed waypoint.

Example of dead reckoning along a predetermined route

Prior to this trip, you calculated the number of steps it takes you to cover 100 m by walking three laps around a standard 400-m running track. You require 1837 steps to cover the 1200 m distance. Your average number of steps to cover 100 m is therefore 1837/12 = 153 steps/100 m. This number reflects the nominal number of steps you need to cover 100 m on hard, flat terrain with no obstructions. In the wilderness, your actual number steps per 100 m will vary depending on how much weight you are carrying, the slope angle, how tired you are, the vegetation density, the snow pack, and many other factors.

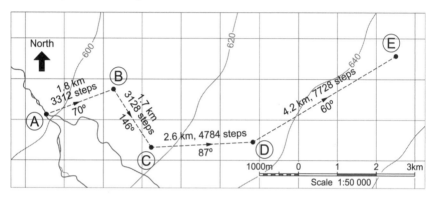

Your starting position on this journey is a creek fork that is easy to identify. You label this position as (A), and plot your route on the map as a sequence of straight-line segments with additional waypoints at (B), (C), (D), and (E). Based on the type of terrain, you decide to increase your nominal step count by 20% for all segments. Your step count becomes 1.2 x 153 = 184 steps/100 m.

With a ruler, measure the length of each segment on the map. The segment distances are 36, 34, 52, and 84 mm. Multiply these numbers by the map scale (1:50 000) to get real world distances. For example, the distance of the first segment is 36 mm x 50 000 = 1 800 000 mm = 1.8 km. Convert this distance to steps: 1.8 km = 1800 m x (184 steps/100 m) = 3312 steps. Calculate and write down the number of steps for each segment. Adjust the declination on your compass so that it conforms to grid north. Take compass bearings off the map between all adjacent waypoints and write down the bearings.

At your starting point (A), set the compass bearing to 70°. Follow this bearing while counting steps. If you encounter obstacles, use detour techniques to avoid losing your step count. Stop when the step count reaches 3312.

At (B), set your compass to 146°, and follow this bearing for 3128 steps to (C). Continue to (D) by following 87° and a count of 4784, and then to your final destination (E) with a bearing of 60° and 7728 steps. The further you travel the more inaccurate your position estimate will be. An excellent method for testing your dead reckoning ability is to retrace your route by following reverse bearings to your start point.

Estimating your position by dead reckoning

Sometimes you cannot plot your route ahead of time because the route is flexible or uncertain. Starting from a known position, keep track of your bearings and travel distances to estimate your dead reckoning position. This is a standard step in sextant navigation. On the ocean, currents and winds will distort your actual speed and bearing. Use mathematical or graphical methods to calculate your dead reckoning position. Graphical methods only work with charts or maps made from conformal projections where the scale at any one point is the same in all directions.

Example of estimating your position by dead reckoning

During a transoceanic sailing trip, you take two sights with a sextant and calculate your position as 47°01'N, 139°08'W. From here, you point the bow of your boat toward a magnetic bearing of 107° for six hours, and then want to establish your dead reckoning position. The magnetic declination is 18°E, and you are using a conformal Mercator chart.

The estimated average forward speed of your boat is 5 knots. By looking at the wake of your boat, you calculate that a steady wind from the southwest causes your boat to drift at a rate of 1 knot in the wind direction (27° magnetic). There is also an ocean current pushing you eastward (72° magnetic) by 1 knot. One knot is defined as one nautical mile per hour. Use the bar scale to find out how long one nautical mile (nm) is on your chart. You could also do this without a bar scale because 1 nm is nearly equivalent to 1' of latitude. On your chart, 1 nm is one fifth of the distance between the latitudes marked 50' and 55', for example.

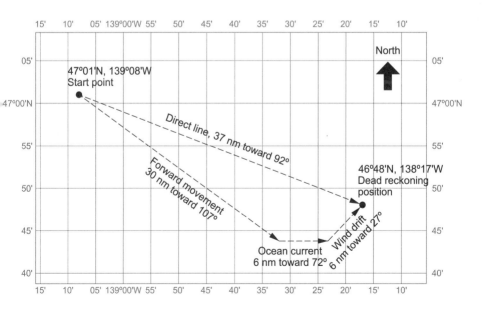

Your net movement from the last known position is a superposition of the movements caused by the boat's forward speed, the ocean current, and the wind drift. After six hours, your boat has moved a distance of 30 nm toward a magnetic bearing of 107°, 6 nm toward 72° (east), and 6 nm toward 27° (northeast). With a plotting tool, draw a line, 30 nm long, from your start point toward a magnetic bearing of 107°. Draw a second line, 6 nm long, from the end of the first line toward 72°, and finally a third line, 6 nm long, from the end of the second line toward 27°. Your dead reckoning position is at the end of the third line. Reading this point off the chart gives a position of 46°48'N, 138°17'W.

For future reference, calculate your actual bearing and ground speed from the start point. On the chart, measure the length of the direct line between your start point and your dead reckoning position. Converting to real world units gives a true distance of 37 nm. Dividing this distance by 6 hours gives a true speed of 6.2 knots. Using the compass rose to measure the bearing of the direct line gives a magnetic bearing of 92°.

8.4 Navigating with map, compass, and altimeter

On land, an altimeter can significantly increase the navigation power of a map and compass. Your movement is guided by conventional map and compass techniques, with the altimeter tracking your progress and helping you pinpoint your location. Take into account all the factors that can distort your altimeter reading (Section 3.3). To keep your altimeter as accurate as possible, calibrate it every time you come across a known elevation on your route.

1. If your compass is equipped with an adjustable magnetic declination mechanism, adjust the declination so that it conforms to grid north. If not, add or subtract the declination after taking each map or field bearing.

2. Find your present location on the map. You may be able to do this by triangulating your position with your altimeter and compass (Section 3.4).

3. Plot a proposed route on your map and mark all critical locations as waypoints. If possible, choose catching features that will help you find the waypoints.

4. Take a compass bearing off the map from your present location to the first way-point. If your first waypoint is on a catching feature, add or subtract a deliberate offset to your bearing.

5. Follow the compass bearing toward your target. Alternatively, you may be able to follow a linear feature. In the latter case, the compass bearing is only used to confirm that you're moving in the correct general direction. If you're traveling up or down a major slope, track your progress by matching the contour lines on the map with your altimeter reading.

6. When you reach the catching feature, follow it to your first waypoint. An altimeter reading will help you verify that you have reached the waypoint.

7. Repeat Step 4 - 6 for subsequent waypoints.

Example of map, compass, and altimeter navigation

You intend to climb and traverse a nearby mountain from a campsite by a lake (A). Your proposed route goes up a gully (B) to the mountain's south ridge (C), which you will follow to the summit (D). Your descent will follow the mountain's north ridge to a fork (E), and then along the northwest ridge to the top of a gully (F). After descending to the bottom of the gully (G), the route goes back to your campsite (A).

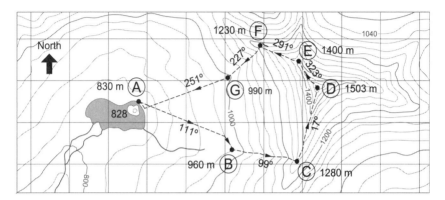

Pinpoint your campsite on the map. This is easy because you are right by the lakeshore and there is an island across from your camp. According to your map, the lake elevation is 828 m. Since your campsite is 2 m above the lake, calibrate your altimeter to 830 m.

Adjust the declination on your compass so that it conforms to grid north. Take a compass bearing off the map from the campsite (A) to the bottom of the gully (B). This gives a bearing of 116°. Subtract a deliberate offset of 5° for an adjusted bearing of 111° to ensure that you end up slightly left of the gully bottom. Your catching feature is the 960 m contour line, the elevation of (B). Follow the 111° bearing until your altimeter reads 960 m. Turn right and travel at a constant elevation to the bottom of the gully (B).

Climb up the gully to the ridge crest, which is at an elevation of 1280 m (C). Follow the ridge to the summit (D). As you climb the ridge, keep track of your progress by checking your altimeter. At the summit, calibrate your altimeter to read 1503 m. Take a bearing off the map from the summit (D) toward the ridge fork (E). As you leave the summit, follow this bearing (323°) to ensure that you are about to go down the correct ridge. Carefully monitor your altimeter as you descend. Keep an eye out for the ridge fork when you approach the 1400-m level.

When you reach the fork (E), take a bearing off the map toward (F). This bearing (291°) should line up with the general direction of the northwest ridge. Descend the northwest ridge. Scout out the terrain to your left as you approach the 1230-m level to ensure that you don't overshoot the gully (F). A bearing from (F) to (G) gives 227°. Use this bearing to confirm that you're about to go down the correct gully. Down-climb the gully to its bottom at 990 m (G). From here, take a bearing to your campsite (256°). Subtract a deliberate offset of 5° for an adjusted bearing of 251°. This will ensure that you hit the lake to the left of your campsite. When you reach the lake, turn right and follow the shoreline to your campsite (A).

8.5 Navigating with map, compass, and GPS

A map, compass, and GPS receiver is a powerful combination. It allows you to navigate through featureless terrain and during poor visibility. With a GPS receiver, you can follow a direct line to a waypoint without worrying about catching features. There are two major techniques: (1) pre-entering waypoints into the receiver, and then navigating along the route with the receiver and compass, or (2) using the receiver to pinpoint your position on the map, and then navigating with conventional map and compass techniques.

Expect some loss of precision whenever you transfer a waypoint from a GPS receiver to a map or vice versa. Normally, the most accurate waypoints in the receiver's memory are the ones acquired from satellite fixes. Consequently, the most accurate bearings displayed by the receiver are those between two satellite-acquired waypoints. A bearing between one manually-entered and one satellite-acquired waypoint is less accurate. The least accurate bearings are between two manually entered waypoints, which are as accurate as a compass bearing taken off a map.

8.5.1 Navigating with pre-entered waypoints

With pre-entered waypoints, just follow the route that you've already stored in the GPS receiver. The receiver tells you the bearing and distance to the next waypoint. The compass points you in the direction of this bearing.

1. If your compass is equipped with an adjustable magnetic declination mechanism, adjust the declination so that it conforms to grid north, and set the GPS receiver to display grid bearings. If your compass lacks an adjustable declination mechanism, set the receiver to display magnetic bearings.

2. At the start of your trip, switch on the receiver and wait for a position fix. If the receiver fails to obtain a fix within a few minutes, the satellite signals are probably blocked by obstructions. Move to a spot where more sky is visible.

3. Make the receiver display the bearing and distance to the first pre-entered waypoint along the route. Turn the graduated dial of the compass to this bearing and switch off the receiver.

4. Follow the compass bearing toward the waypoint. Anytime you suspect you're off route, switch on the GPS receiver. After acquiring fix, make the receiver redisplay the distance and bearing to the waypoint. Adjust the compass to this new bearing.

5. Once you reach the first waypoint, repeat Step 2 - 4 for subsequent waypoints along the route.

This method doesn't strictly require you to look at the map after the waypoints have been entered, but you should to do it anyway. If you don't look at the map, you will have difficulty accessing the terrain and may run into unexpected obstacles.

Example of navigating with pre-entered waypoints

The example in Section 4.8.1 shows how to transfer waypoints from a map to a GPS receiver. You are now ready to follow this route in the real world.

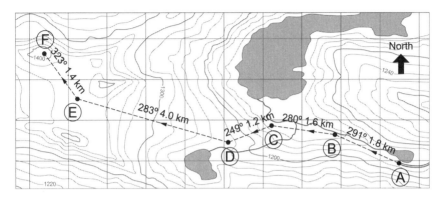

Your trip begins at the end of a road, a position that you have already pre-entered into your receiver as waypoint (A). Switch on the receiver, wait for a position fix, and compare the result with the pre-entered waypoint. This will tell you how accurate you were at transferring (A) from the map to your receiver. Update waypoint (A) with the numbers from your acquired fix. Set the GPS receiver to display grid bearings and read off the magnetic declination. Let's say the receiver shows that the declination relative to the grid is 28°E. Set the declination mechanism on your compass to 28°E. If your compass doesn't have a declination mechanism, set the GPS receiver to display magnetic bearings.

The receiver tells you that (B) is 1.8 km away at a grid bearing of 291° or a magnetic bearing of 263°. Set your compass to 291° if it has a declination mechanism (263° if it doesn't). Switch off the receiver and follow the compass bearing to (B). If you lose track of your location along the way, switch on the receiver, make it display the distance and bearing to (B), set your compass to this new bearing, and follow the bearing toward (B).

Use the same procedure to navigate to subsequent waypoints: follow 280° (or magnetic 252°) for 1.6 km to (C); 249° (221°) for 1.2 km to (D); 283° (255°) for 4.0 km to (E), and 323° (295°) for 1.4 km to (F). Note that you do not necessarily have to reach the exact location of each pre-entered waypoint. If you are planning to return by the same route, replace each pre-entered waypoint with an acquired position fix.

8.5.2 Navigating without pre-entered waypoints

Without pre-entered waypoints, the GPS receiver is just a powerful accessory to conventional map and compass navigation. Use the receiver only when you're unsure of your position.

1. Switch on the GPS receiver. Make sure that the receiver is set to the same grid system and datum as your map. Wait for a position fix.

2. Use the map's grid or geographic coordinates to pinpoint your position on the map.

3. Take a compass bearing off the map from your current position toward your next target. Follow this bearing toward your target.

8.6 Navigating without maps

You may for some reason decide to venture into unfamiliar territory without a map. This type of excursion is considered exploratory since you don't really know what lies beyond your range of view. Even with a guidebook or a verbal description of the area, you will lack the detailed terrain information that only a good map can provide. Finding your way back to your starting point should be your main navigational concern. Your strategy is governed by the terrain features that you encounter during your outgoing journey and what navigation tools you have at your disposal.

8.6.1 Navigating with nothing

A surprising number of people head out into untracked wilderness with neither a map nor any other navigation tools. Most who do this somehow manage to find their way back, although not necessarily along a return route that offers the greatest likelihood of success. Memorize all the significant landmarks that you come across during your outgoing journey, and frequently look back to familiarize yourself with the opposing view. During your return trip, use the memorized landmarks as steering marks to keep you on track.

Estimate the orientation of the cardinal directions before heading off. This can be done by observing the sun if it is visible (Section 5.2). Keep track of rough directions as you travel. If you encounter a large terrain feature, determine whether it tends north-south, east-west, or some other intermediate direction. Travel along, or parallel to, linear features that happen to be aligned with your desired travel direction. During your return journey, follow the same linear features or choose travel directions that will lead you to catching features that you are unlikely to miss. After reaching a catching feature, follow its perimeter to an identifiable point and then aim for the next catching feature.

Example of navigating with nothing

You decide to explore a trackless wilderness adjacent to a road, even though you know little about the terrain and have neither a map nor any other navigation tools. Your game plan is to head straight east from the road and continue traveling in that direction unless you're forced to circumvent obstacles. For your return, you intend to reverse your general travel direction by heading west, and use catching features to find intermediate locations.

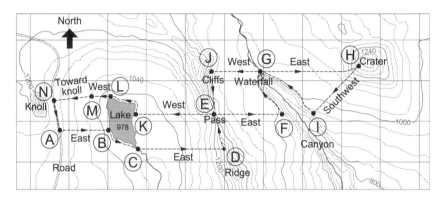

After parking your vehicle at (A), you head east from the road by using the sun and your clock to estimate your bearing. Your first obstacle is a lake that you bump into at (B). Going counterclockwise along the lakeshore guides you to its outlet at (C). From here, you continue eastward until you gain a ridge crest at (D). Following the ridge crest northward leads to a pass at (E), from where you resume your eastward journey. Your next obstacle is a canyon (F), which you circumvent by going left along its perimeter until the canyon terminates near a waterfall at (G). Carrying on eastward, you spot a volcanic crater and decide that this feature will be your final destination.

After reaching the crater rim at (H), you work out a navigation strategy for your return. You intend to navigate back via points (G), (E), and (C), which are easy to find, and ignore the nondescript points (F), (D), and (B). Your chief catching features are going to be the canyon wall, the cliff bands north of the pass, the lake, and the road.

To ensure that you hit the canyon, start hiking southwest instead of west. After reaching the canyon wall at (I), follow the perimeter of the canyon to the waterfall (G). From here, go straight west until you reach the base of the cliffs at (J). Follow the cliffs southward to the pass (E), and then take a westward course to the lake, which you hit at (K). You decide to ignore (C) because you're closer to the north end of the lake, and instead go counterclockwise along the lakeshore to (L) where you resume your westward travel. At (M) you spot a knoll that you recognize from when you parked your vehicle. Head straight toward the knoll until you reach the road at (N). Go south along the road back to your vehicle.

8.6.2 Navigating with just a compass

Navigating with just a compass is a step up from navigating with nothing. It gives you more precise directions than the sun or other natural clues. Aside from memorizing the terrain, your primary navigation concern is recording what bearings you have followed during your outgoing journey. Your return strategy is the same as for navigating with nothing except that the increased directional accuracy of your compass allows you to aim toward narrower catching features.

Example of navigating with just a compass

You decide to explore the same trackless wilderness as in the previous example, but this time you have a compass. Instead of going straight east, you plan to head off perpendicular to the road and keep traveling in that direction unless blocked by obstacles. For your return you will follow the reverse compass bearing as much as possible.

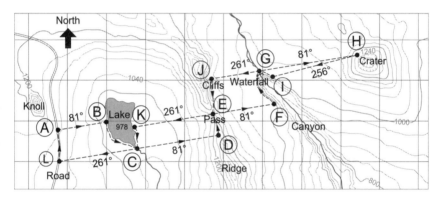

At (A), you take a compass bearing perpendicular to the road, resulting in a bearing of 81°. Following this bearing takes you to the lake at (B), and hiking along the lakeshore leads to its outlet at (C). From here, you continue along your original bearing of 81° until you gain the crest of the ridge at (D). The ridge crest takes you to the pass at (E). You continue along your original bearing to the canyon, which you reach at (F). Following the canyon perimeter brings you to the waterfall at (G). Lastly, you gain the crater rim at (H) by following your original 81° bearing.

Your chief catching features for the return are the same as for the previous example: the canyon wall, cliffs, lake, and road. Adding 180° to your original bearing gives you a return bearing of 261°. To ensure that you don't miss the canyon, subtract a deliberate offset of 5° and follow a bearing of 256°. After reaching the canyon at (I), follow its rim to the waterfall at (G). The reverse bearing (261°) then takes you to the cliffs at (J). Go southward below the cliffs until you reach the pass at (E). From the pass, follow the reverse compass bearing to the lake, which you encounter at (K). Go left along the lakeshore to the outlet at (C). The last target is the road, a long linear feature that is hard to miss. Follow the reverse bearing to (L) and then go north along the road to your vehicle.

8.6.3 Navigating with just a GPS receiver and compass

A GPS receiver and a compass is a powerful combination for backtracking along a previously traveled route. The technique is simple and effective. Mark certain critical locations as waypoints in your receiver during your outgoing journey. On your return, use the receiver and compass to navigate back via these same waypoints. You can travel directly toward a waypoint without following linear features or aiming for catching features. Be aware that your GPS receiver may not work in canyons or under heavy tree cover.

1. At the start of your trip, switch on your receiver and wait for a position fix. If your receiver fails to obtain a fix within a few minutes move to a location where more sky is visible. Save the position fix in the receiver's memory as a waypoint and then switch off the receiver.

2. Each time you come across a critical juncture, switch on the receiver and save this position as another waypoint. Organize the waypoints sequentially into an electronic route.

3. Before starting your return trip, adjust the declination on your compass so that it conforms to true north, and set the GPS receiver to display true bearings. If your compass lacks an adjustable declination mechanism, set the receiver to display magnetic bearings.

4. At the start of your return trip, switch on your receiver and wait for a position fix. Make the receiver display the bearing and distance to the last waypoint that you saved on your outgoing journey. Turn the graduated dial on your compass to the bearing shown on the receiver. Switch off your receiver and follow your compass bearing toward the waypoint.

5. Once you reach the waypoint, repeat Step 4 for subsequent waypoints until you return to your starting point.

Example of GPS and compass navigation

You decide to explore the same wilderness as the in two previous examples. Your strategy for the outgoing trip is the same as with just a compass; head off perpendicular to the road and keep traveling in that direction unless blocked by obstacles. You will mark all critical locations as waypoints in your receiver.

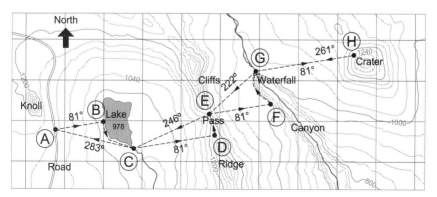

Before leaving, acquire a position fix at (A) and save it as a waypoint. Taking a compass bearing perpendicular to the road gives you the same bearing of 81° as in the previous example. Your journey follows the same path to the crater. Along the way, you save critical locations (C), (E), and (G) as waypoints in your GPS receiver, while ignoring the unimportant points (B), (D), and (F).

When you are ready to return, acquire a position fix and make the receiver display the bearing to the waterfall at (G). Set your compass to this bearing (261°) and follow the bearing directly toward (G). If you have trouble finding the waterfall, acquire another position fix and make the receiver redisplay the bearing to the waterfall. Readjust your compass to the new bearing and follow this bearing to the waterfall. Use the same technique to navigate to the pass at (E) by following a bearing of 222°. Similarly, follow a bearing of 246° to the lake outlet at (C) and a bearing of 283° directly to your vehicle at (A).

8.7 Real life navigation

Given that there are so many methods at your disposal, how should you navigate in real life? You are confronted with two conflicting factors: efficiency, and assurance of success. Efficient travel means doing the minimum amount of navigating that you think is necessary, while making sure that you find your destination may require a lot of extra work. A skilled navigator balances these two factors and switches navigation techniques as circumstances change. For example, you could use efficient terrain association to keep track of your location when landmarks are visible, then switch to time consuming dead reckoning when the landmarks disappear from view.

Judging when it's appropriate to use a particular navigation method is something that comes with experience. Depending on the situation, the outcomes from certain methods will be more credible than others. If in doubt, choose the method that gives you the best chance of success. The time saved by using an efficient navigation method will be quickly eaten up if you do a mistake.

8.8 Lost in the wilderness

Consider yourself lost if you don't know which way to proceed and are unsure of how to backtrack. Stop immediately unless you are in an unsafe location, in which case continue to the nearest safe location. Then relax, have something to eat or drink, and take some time to evaluate your situation. The key is not to panic. Calmly ask yourself the following questions:

- How badly lost am I really? How long ago did I know where I was going?

- What navigation tools, if any, do I have at my disposal?

- Do the visibility, weather, and other conditions allow safe travel?

- Have I informed someone about the details of my planned outing before heading out? The best information to leave at home or in your vehicle is a map with your intended route drawn in.

- Do I have a means to communicate with civilization?

- Am I in a part of the world where a rescue is likely, and if so, how long would I expect to wait for searchers to find me? Do I have the means to survive until then? Without a communication device, it may take a long time before you're found. First, someone has to determine that you need help, then he or she has to contact the authorities that have to launch a search, and finally, the searchers have to find you.

Based on your answers, make a rational decision whether to stay put and wait for a rescue or try to find your way out under your own power. Take into account that you will need more food and water while traveling than if you stay in one location. In most cases, it is easier for rescuers to find someone who stays in one place.

8.8.1 Waiting for a rescue

You are faced with two important but potentially conflicting considerations if you decide to wait for a rescue: how to survive and how to attract attention.

- Survival often means seeking shelter under a rock or tree where it is hard for rescuers to spot you, while making yourself visible means exposing yourself to the elements. A way around this dilemma is to seek shelter near a location where you can quickly make yourself visible.

- Leave as many clues as possible about of your presence. Mark the nearby ground with rescue signals and with any bright equipment or clothing that you are not wearing.

- Make sure that all available signaling devices, such as mirrors, flashlights, whistles, flares, or fires are ready for immediate deployment. Do not hesitate to use any of your visual signaling devices if you spot a low flying aircraft. Respond promptly to any attempt by rescuers to contact you.

- If you have an electronic communication device, use it to call for help. Remember that certain types of radios work better at night than during the day, and certain locations may have much better reception than other nearby locations.

- If you decide to move to a new location, leave as many clues as possible of your movement. Use techniques such as deliberately planting footprints into the ground or marking your route with symbols.

- Most rescue professionals recommend that all members of a group stay together. This doesn't necessarily mean that you must all wait at exactly the same spot. In some cases, spreading the group over an area can enhance the probability of one member being found. If you decide to spread out, make sure that everyone knows where all the other members are located.

- Do not approach a helicopter unless its engines are turned off or the pilot signals that it's safe.

8.8.2 Finding your way out

The standard method for finding your way out is to backtrack until you come across terrain that you recognize. Many people have successfully used this technique, but it is not always an option. The visibility may have deteriorated, nightfall is imminent, or you have traveled too far to turn around. In some cases, backtracking means traveling uphill, upstream, or against the wind. Another concern is that you could end up even more lost and further away from the area where potential rescuers would search.

If the travel conditions are unfavorable, waiting for better conditions can dramatically improve your prospects of finding your way out in a safe manner. You have a good chance of finding your way out if you're surrounded by landmarks and have a map and compass.

1. If your view is obstructed, move to a nearby location with better view, such as, a hilltop, clearing, or lakeshore. Try to identify any visible landmarks, and if possible, determine your position by terrain association or compass triangulation.

2. If terrain association or compass triangulation fails because of poor visibility or lack of identifiable landmarks, draw a circle on your map with a radius equal to the estimated distance from your last known location and centered on your last known location. A reasonable assumption is that you're somewhere within this circle.

3. Use your compass to orient the map and then systematically study the surrounding terrain and the contour lines on your map within the circle. Narrow down your possible locations within the circle by eliminating all areas that don't make sense. For example, if you're on flat ground, eliminate all areas that show steep terrain. Then identify locations within the circle that look like logical candidates for your position.

4. On the map, select a large catching feature such as a river, lake, ridge, or power line that looks like a reasonable target to aim for. Take a compass bearing from the middle of your location candidates toward the selected feature. Check that the same bearing will bring you to the catching feature from all location candidates. If not, select a larger catching feature or try to eliminate more of your location candidates.

5. Once you've taken a bearing that is sure to hit the catching feature from any of your location candidates, follow that bearing until you reach the catching feature. Now it's just a matter of determining your position on the catching feature. If you can identify one visible landmark, use triangulation from a linear feature to determine your position.

6. If you cannot identify any landmarks, move along the feature until you see a suitable landmark, or come across a uniquely identifiable part of the catching feature itself. You are then no longer lost.

You can use a similar procedure without a compass but must instead use natural methods such as the sun to estimate directions and orient the map. Since these alternate methods are normally less accurate than a compass, aim for an even larger catching feature. Without a map, use your memory of the terrain to select appropriate targets. Keep in mind that traveling in the correct general direction is more important than knowing where you are.

8.9 Rhumb lines and great circle routes

For very long journeys across wide-open spaces, there are techniques for minimizing the travel distance between two locations that are far apart. A rhumb line is a route between two points that follows a constant bearing. Rhumb lines are straight lines on Mercator charts, but are not usually the shortest distance between two points. To travel along a rhumb line, simply take a bearing off a Mercator chart from your current position to your destination, and then follow that bearing to your destination. Calculating the real world distance along a rhumb line is complicated because the scale varies across the chart. The easiest method is to use a computer program.

A great circle route is the shortest path along Earth's surface between any two points. Great circle routes look like arcs on Mercator charts. The easiest way to visualize a great circle route is to stretch a string between two points on a globe. In general, a great circle route doesn't follow a constant compass bearing. You must continually readjust your compass bearing to stay on course. The only exception to this rule occurs when a great circle route coincides with a rhumb line, which happens only when you travel along a longitude or the equator.

Plotting a great circle route is mathematically complex and is best done on a gnomonic chart or with a computer program. Gnomonic charts are created with a projection that shows great circle routes as straight lines. The task of following a great circle route becomes much easier if you don't plot the route in advance, but instead do it as you travel. By default, a GPS receiver displays the distance and initial bearing to a waypoint along a great circle route. Similarly, in sextant navigation, the sight reduction tables give you an initial bearing that follows a great circle route. By frequently recalculating your position and the bearing toward your destination, you will automatically be guided along a great circle route. The difference in length between a great circle route and a rhumb line is insignificant in most navigation situations except at high latitudes or on very long journeys with large east-west displacements.

Example of rhumb line versus great circle route

Let's say you're planning to row a dinghy from Saint John's, Newfoundland (47°34'N, 52°42'W) to Kilkee, Ireland (52°41'N, 9°38'W), and are wondering whether to follow a great circle route or a rhumb line.

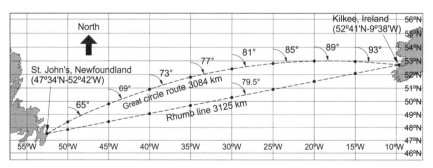

Taking a bearing from Saint John's to Kilkee on a Mercator chart gives you a true bearing of 79.5°. You can theoretically follow this bearing directly to your destination. Plugging the coordinates of St. John's and Kilkee into a navigation calculator gives a rhumb line distance of 3125 km. Plugging the same coordinates into a GPS receiver gives a great circle distance of 3084 km and an initial bearing of 63°. The great circle route reduces your distance by 41 km, but the navigation becomes more convoluted. By the time you reach 48°27'N, 50°00'W, the bearing to Kilkee will have changed to 65°. From here, you must increase your bearing by about 4° for every 5° of longitude that you cross. Your bearing will be 97° as you approach Kilkee.

In practice, your travel route is governed by prevailing winds and currents rather than by meticulously trying to follow a rhumb line or a great circle route.

8.10 Route finding

Route finding is defined as selecting a viable route across whatever terrain you are traveling. It is often confused with navigation, but is really a separate topic that is more difficult to master than pure navigation. Route finding is critical for safe wilderness travel and requires solid knowledge of the type of terrain you're dealing with. Deciding if a proposed route is feasible depends on whether you and your travel companions have the necessary technical skills, fitness levels, and equipment to safely negotiate the route.

Route finding usually involves several stages. The first step is to study maps or charts, and then trace out a route that looks doable. In mountainous terrain, calculate the average angles of the steepest slopes along your proposed route to find out if these slopes are too steep for your abilities. Remember that real slopes have sections that are steeper than the average. Large-scale maps with small contour intervals are best for calculating slopes and picking out details. Check out pictures or aerial photos of critical sections, or talk to someone who has previously done your intended route.

Once you arrive in the area, consult with the local experts. They can provide valuable insight on present conditions, weather patterns, features not shown on maps, and pitfalls to avoid. Every part of the world has its own particular type of climate, geology, vegetation, and even wildlife that can influence your route selection. You will likely have to re-evaluate your route as you travel. Having done your homework, any changes will hopefully be minor. If you're unsure if a proposed route is viable, try scouting it out first. Features often look and feel much different close up or from a new vantage point.

A whole spectrum of outdoor activities require route finding skills. Climbing a rock face obviously requires different route finding skills than bushwhacking through a jungle, negotiating a crevasse field, or kayaking down a raging river. There is no substitute for experience when it comes to mastering the intricacies of route finding. It cannot be learned by reading a book. The quickest way to improve your route finding ability is to team-up with an experienced outdoor person who is familiar with the local terrain and has the required technical skills for the particular activity. Every time you encounter a choice of routes, ask why a particular route was chosen rather than another. And most importantly, take advantage of any opportunities to practice your own route finding.

Chapter 9
Scenarios

Anyone who spends enough time in the wilderness will sooner or later have to deal with various navigation challenges. Fortunately, almost any navigation problem is solvable with the proper tools, skills, and sometimes, a touch of ingenuity. The following scenarios describe both common and unusual things that you may encounter.

9.1 Trail switchbacks

After hiking up a well-maintained trail through several switchbacks, the trail abruptly turns rough and then completely disappears. You are wondering what happened to the trail. It was supposed to be in excellent condition.

A missed switchback is the most likely cause of your predicament. Going straight at a switchback is so common that a trail is sometimes worn into the ground by hikers who have missed the switchback. If a good trail suddenly turns rough, stop and retrace your steps to find out if you are in fact on the proper trail. Better yet, fight the natural tendency to look down at your feet or blindly follow the person ahead of you.

Continually scan the terrain left and right as you travel and periodically look back at the view behind you. Look at distant landmarks or use your compass to confirm that the trail is going in the correct general direction.

9.2 Multiple ski tracks

You are skiing back to your vehicle after a day of skiing in a popular backcountry ski area. On your way down a broad ridge, you encounter numerous ski tracks, and argue with your partner about which tracks to follow.

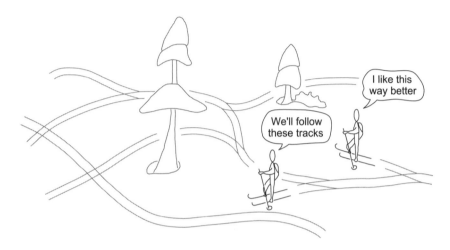

Skiers traveling uphill usually try to avoid extra effort by following a track that is already there. On the other hand, skiers traveling downhill in open terrain tend to seek out untracked snow, creating many tracks dispersed across the terrain. As a result, you will usually encounter more downhill tracks than uphill tracks in a busy area.

Uphill travel is slower and technically easier, allowing the skier who creates the track more time for navigation and route finding. Uphill tracks are therefore less likely to lead you astray, and often terminate at a popular destination such as a cabin or parking area. If you come across a web of ski tracks, your best bet is to follow a well-used set of uphill tracks, regardless whether you are traveling uphill or downhill.

Before following any track, make sure that it runs in the general direction where you want to go. Take a compass bearing off your map to confirm the direction. If you come across a major fork in the track, pinpoint your position on the map, and then use your compass to decide which track follow.

9.3 Shoreline travel direction

During a leisurely canoe circuit, you decide to pull ashore and climb a distant hill. You haul your canoe to shore and then hike to the top of the hill in a few hours. After returning to the lake, you go left along the shoreline but then decide that the canoe must instead be to your right. After seesawing back and forth a few times, you still haven't found the canoe.

The lakeshore is an extensive linear feature that is easy to find, while the canoe is a point feature that is much harder to find. It therefore makes sense to first find the lakeshore and then follow the shoreline to the canoe. You must however plan ahead so that you know which direction to go once you reach the lake. Several methods will accomplish this.

Use your compass to take a field bearing off a landmark before leaving the canoe. The landmark could be something across the lake or an island in the lake. Write down the compass bearing. When you return to the lakeshore, aim your compass in the direction of the landmark's bearing. Travel in whatever direction that will make the bearing point closer to the landmark. You should be very close to the canoe when the compass bearing points directly toward the landmark.

If you cannot see any obvious landmarks from the shoreline, take a field bearing off the hill itself before starting your hike. When you reach the top of the hill, reverse your bearing by adding or subtracting 180° from your original bearing. Then, add or subtract a deliberate offset of a few degrees. Follow the offset bearing to the lake. When you reach the shoreline, the canoe will be to your right (facing the lake) if your deliberate offset was subtracted, and to your left if your deliberate offset was added.

Another option is to mark the canoe's location as a waypoint in a GPS receiver. On your return, use the receiver and compass to travel directly toward the canoe. If you don't find the canoe when you reach the shoreline, use your GPS receiver to redisplay the bearing and distance to the canoe. You should be able to acquire a position fix quite easily along the shoreline where a significant amount of sky is visible.

9.4 Mountain top triangulation

Lost in the fog with just a map and compass, you decide to scramble up a nearby knoll. The fog suddenly clears as you reach the top where you are blessed with a panoramic view of several mountains sticking up above the clouds.

This is a classic situation where you can use compass triangulation to pinpoint your location. First, orient the map, and then try to identify at least two of the visible mountains by carefully comparing the shape of the mountains with the contour lines on the map. This can be tricky if only a small part of each mountain is visible. If the upper boundary of the cloud cover is fairly level, judge how far the visible part of each mountain sticks up above the clouds. Rank the mountains by height, and then compare the observed heights with the elevations on the map. You may be able to immediately identify the knoll that you are standing on by its position and height relative to the mountains.

To triangulate your position, take a field bearing off one of the peaks and draw a line of position on your map. Take a field bearing off a second mountain and use this bearing to draw a second line of position. If you have done the triangulation properly, you are located at the intersection between the two lines of position. Take bearings off additional mountains for greater confidence in your result.

After pinpointing your position, take a compass bearing off the map toward your next catching feature. Make sure that the catching feature is sufficiently large so that you will not miss it if you drift off course after descending into the fog.

9.5 Hidden trail markers

You're hiking along an easy-to-follow trail that is marked with reflective markers attached to trees. Higher up, you encounter snow and strap on your snowshoes. The trail markers eventually vanish under the increasingly deeper snow cover, and you suddenly realize that you have no idea where the trail goes.

This is a situation where the navigation abruptly changes from casual to challenging. The trail is no longer a linear feature that you can easily follow. If you're not carrying a map and compass, turn back before you get lost. Do not count on being able to retrace your tracks, as they could melt away or get covered by new snow.

Finding the location of the last visible trail marker is vital for your return trip. If landmarks are visible, use your compass to triangulate this location and record the bearings. Alternatively, mark the location as an altimeter reading or GPS waypoint. Because of the possibility of a forced retreat, mark this location even if you intend to return via a different route.

Once past the last trail marker, your navigation is governed by whether landmarks are visible and what navigation tools you have. For example, if the terrain is allows, you could use conventional map and compass techniques.

9.6 Jungle camp

Your plan to find a remote camp in the Amazon jungle with a GPS receiver has failed because the satellite signals cannot penetrate the thick tree canopy. The vegetation also blocks your view of landmarks, preventing you from triangulating your position with a compass.

Use your map, compass, and altimeter as primary navigation tools as these will work under tree cover. Carefully plan your intended route before leaving. Break up the route into segments, with an intermediate catching feature at the end of each segment. A catching feature can be a lake, river, hill, swamp, or an elevation that matches a contour line on your map. Take advantage of any openings in the tree cover to get a GPS reading or to triangulate your position.

The illustration below shows an example of jungle navigation. From your start point, take a bearing off your map toward your first catching feature, the center of a lake. Follow the bearing to the lake. Walk to the end of the lake and take a bearing to your second catching feature, the center of a hill. After reaching the hill and going around its base, take a bearing to your last catching feature, a river fork. Add a deliberate offset of a few degrees to your bearing and follow this offset bearing to the river. Go upstream along the river to the fork. The jungle camp is away from obvious landmarks, so you are forced to use dead reckoning for this last leg. A final grid search may be needed to find the camp.

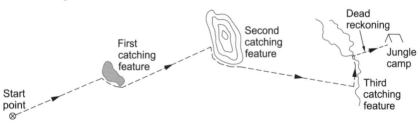

Dead reckoning is not easy in a jungle. The thick undergrowth makes it difficult to walk in a straight line while keeping track of your distance by counting paces. The most common error is to grossly overestimate your travel distance. With experience, you will be able to use your travel time to estimate the distance. Keep in mind that jungles are not always accurately mapped because the heavy tree cover makes aerial surveying difficult.

9.7 Ridge return

After scrambling up a face to reach a ridge, you follow the ridge to the top of a hill. On your return from the hill, you descend along the same ridge but miss the turnoff, and instead continue further down the ridge into unfamiliar terrain, wondering how you got off route.

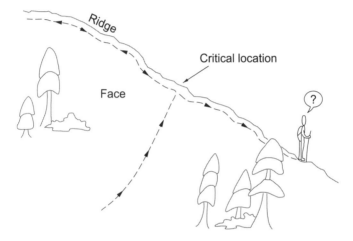

The natural tendency is to look straight ahead as you travel. It is very easy to miss a right-angle turn off a ridge, especially if there are no distinctive terrain features nearby. Once you realize that you have gone too far, go back up the ridge and find the point where your route leaves the ridge. This is a critical location that you should have memorized on your way up, and marked as a GPS waypoint, altimeter reading, or by recording triangulation bearings.

Alternatively, place a line of wands or cairns perpendicular to your line of travel at this critical juncture. A cairn is simply a stone marker that you build by stacking rocks on top of each other. A wand is a bamboo stick with a small colored flag tied to the top.

9.8 Desert traverse

For your next vacation, you decide on a solo camel trip across the Sahara desert from Tripoli to Timbuktu with various oases along the way. You realize that navigation will be critical to your survival.

The local population has traveled this desert for millennia using celestial bodies, sand dunes, and desert animals for navigation. You on the other hand, should invest in a compass, GPS receiver, and maybe a solar panel to charge the batteries. As a backup, you may want to bring along a sextant, a celestial navigation calculator, and an accurate clock. Before leaving home, pour over maps of the area and write down the coordinates of all the oases along your route. Plan possible escape routes in case you're faced with an emergency.

To navigate your route, simply plug the coordinates of all the oases into your GPS receiver, and then use the receiver and compass to point you toward the next oasis. In this type of terrain your exact path between the oases doesn't really matter. The wide-open terrain offers excellent long-range visibility but sandstorms and mirages can drastically degrade your view. A common mistake is to grossly underestimate distances to visible landmarks.

A long desert trip is an excellent opportunity to practice natural navigation methods. Try using rising and setting stars as direction finders and zenith stars to estimate your latitude. During the day, use the sun and your clock to determine rough directions. Most deserts have seasonal prevailing winds that arrange the sand dunes into specific patterns that you can use to stay on course. You may be able to find an oasis that is beyond your view by observing the movements of desert animals. Knowing the feeding and predator avoidance habits of desert species can help you determine if a particular animal is moving toward or away from an oasis. Desert pigeons, for example, flap their wings louder when flying away from an oasis because they are heavier from drinking water.

9.9 River delta

You set up camp on an island during a long canoe trip down the Mackenzie River delta. After dinner, you head out for a short paddle to explore the nearby channels and islands. On your return, you are unable to find your campsite. There are no obvious landmarks, all channels and islands look the same, and there are no hills to use as vantage points. To make matters worse, your map and all your navigation equipment are left behind in camp.

People habitually treat short excursions with less respect than they should. In this timeless scenario, your food and survival gear is at a campsite that you can't find. Instead of wasting energy on a wild paddling spree hoping to stumble onto the camp, stop and draw up a structured plan for finding your way back. If your camp is nearby you should be able to find it with some kind of grid search.

Devise a method to mark your search route such as breaking branches or building cairns along the shoreline. Clearly mark your start point and then explore one of the nearby channels, marking your route as you go along. Return to your initial marked position and then explore the next channel. Repeat this process until you've covered all the nearby channels. If you haven't found your camp, move to a new base point located on the perimeter of your previous search area and explore outward from this point. Your search area will expand exponentially as you move outward, but a systematic search has huge psychological benefits and is much better than hoping for a miracle. As a last resort, consider abandoning your camp and drifting downstream to the nearest settlement.

As always, prevention is the best medicine. Before setting off, realize that the campsite is a critical location and employ effective methods to retrace your steps. Triangulating your campsite with a compass will not work in this case because there are no obvious landmarks, and an altimeter is useless on a broad, flat delta. Marking the campsite as a waypoint in a GPS receiver is very effective. If you don't have a GPS receiver, devise a method for keeping track of your outward journey. For example, trace your route on the map as you travel or mark the route with cairns. You could also record your journey as a series of compass bearings together with the distance paddled along each bearing. Don't forget to frequently look back to familiarize yourself with the opposing view.

9.10 Descent off mountain

You reach the summit of a remote peak just as the fog rolls in and decide to quickly get off the mountain. Rushing downhill as the fog thickens, you inadvertently veer off to the wrong side of the mountain and find your route blocked by a cliff. Climbing back up to attempt to rejoin your ascent route does not seem viable, as there is now a full-blown storm above.

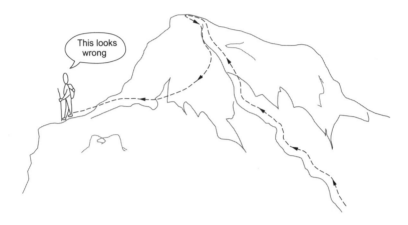

Most people get lost on their way down from mountains, not on their way up. As you climb higher, the overlying terrain decreases in size, effectively funneling you toward the summit. The reverse happens on the descent. You are faced with ever expanding terrain and an increasing number of route choices, each potentially wrong. Rushing downhill during poor visibility is usually a bad idea. Losing your way on the descent can have serious consequences, particularly on high, remote, or technically demanding mountains.

An effective method to retrace your steps is to place wands along your route as you ascend. The wands should be placed close enough so that you can find the next one even if the visibility is drastically reduced. Don't worry if the wands look ridiculously close together. Place extra wands at critical locations such as rappel stations, ridge forks, or crevasse bridges. Also, mark these locations as GPS waypoints, altimeter readings, or by recording triangulation bearings.

If you plan to descend via a different route, carefully research your descent route ahead of time by analyzing maps and photos, consulting a guidebook, or talking to someone who has climbed that route. Note the elevations of all critical locations. Altimeters are particularly valuable for finding critical locations on mountains. Plan for the possibility of a forced retreat down your ascent route. Also, investigate possible escape routes that can get you down quickly in case of an emergency.

9.11 Trail return

You're returning on the same trail that you used to access a wilderness area. For some reason, the trail looks different and seems longer than on the outward journey. You are wondering if you are in fact on the correct trail.

Most people are amazed by how different a trail or any other type of route looks on the return journey. This perception is caused by inattention during the outward journey and altered viewpoints during the return journey. During the outward journey, your mind is naturally focused on the goal at hand, making it easy to forget certain features or having traveled particular sections of the route. This leads to a truncated mental image of the route and many people are surprised by how long it takes to return. This perception is amplified when conditions have changed since your outward journey. For example, it may be darker on your return journey.

The best cure is to familiarize yourself with the opposing view by frequently looking back during your outward journey. This will help you build a more complete mental image of the route. Pay attention to unique features in all directions and mark critical points along your route as GPS waypoints, altimeter readings, by recording triangulation bearings, or with physical markers such as cairns or flagging tape.

9.12 Return to highway

You're driving along the Alaska Highway across flat terrain and decide to check out the local swamps. You head off at a right angle to the highway through low-lying fog. After going straight ahead for a while, you decide to turn back because of the mosquitoes. For some reason the return journey is taking much longer than the outgoing hike and the highway seems to have vanished. As the fog lifts, you notice that the sun is in the wrong direction. You're actually heading away from, instead of toward, the highway.

Terrain that looks the same in all directions can easily deceive your sense of direction. On flat terrain, almost everyone curves consistently to the left or to the right if no distant reference points are in view. The difference in leg lengths is the main cause of this effect. If your right leg is longer, you tend to veer to the left and vice versa. Other factors include having one dominant eye and the tendency to veer downhill and away from the wind. The faster you travel, the more you curve. To determine your innate curving disposition, find a flat area with no obstacles and walk with your eyes closed. If the ground is covered with sand or snow, your footprints will illustrate your personal curving disposition. You can then compensate by consciously forcing yourself to veer in the opposite direction.

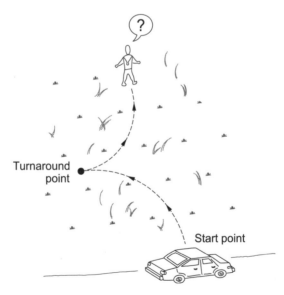

In this scenario, your tendency to veer left eventually altered your travel direction by 90°. On your way back you continued to veer left, ultimately traveling directly opposite to your intended direction. This type of scenario can easily be avoided by using a compass. Before leaving your car, take a compass bearing in the direction that you want to travel and then follow this bearing. For your return journey, add or subtract 180° to your original compass bearing, then add or subtract a deliberate offset of a few degrees. Follow the offset bearing back to the highway, an extensive linear feature that you're unlikely to miss. After arriving at the highway, the deliberate offset will govern which direction to go along the highway to reach your car.

If the sky is clear, you can use the sun to stay on track. Note the direction of the sun as you depart from the car and then keep a course that is at a specific angle relative to the sun. As you travel, slowly adjust your bearing to compensate for the clockwise (counterclockwise in the southern hemisphere) movement of the sun, which averages 15° an hour. Use the same principle to return to the highway.

Returning directly to the spot where your car is parked requires precise navigation. Unless there is a distinct landmark near the car, you'll probably need a GPS receiver. Mark the car as a waypoint before heading off. To find your way back to the car from anywhere in the swamp, just switch on your receiver and make it show the distance and bearing toward the car. Set your compass to this bearing and follow the bearing directly to your car.

9.13 Large group

Thrashing through the wilderness with a large group of people, you suddenly realize that you can't see or hear your friends anymore. You were just tagging along with the rest of the bunch and don't know much about the intended route or the surrounding terrain. To make matters worse, you're carrying neither a map nor a compass, plus the roar of a nearby river drowns out your shouts.

Large groups are notorious for fragmenting into subgroups because of unequal travel speeds. In some cases, one or more members are inadvertently left behind after a rest stop. Ideally, the whole group should stay together as one cohesive unit by traveling at the speed of the slowest member. Unfortunately, this doesn't always happen in practice and often leads to wild speculation about the location of members who are out of sight.

A common predicament occurs when only a few members know the route or have the required navigation skills and equipment. If these members get too far ahead, the group that follows may be forced to second-guess which way to go. A wrong turn will lead the followers astray, while the group on the correct path will be wondering why the followers aren't arriving.

Another type of dilemma arises when one group believes that a second group is ahead when it is in fact behind. The first group speeds up in an attempt to catch up but ends up leaving the second group further behind. Eventually one or both groups may initiate a search, which can degenerate into a ridiculous cat and mouse game with the groups seesawing back and forth along the route, or scattering across the terrain in a desperate attempt to find each other.

Before starting out, all participants must be informed of the proposed route. Predetermined meeting points and what to do if someone becomes separated should be discussed in advance. The leading group must wait at critical junctions, such as trail forks, until the rest of the members catch up or indicate the correct travel direction with markers. Do a body count at each rest stop to ensure that nobody is missing. In a few instances, a group has returned home without realizing that a lost or injured member is still out in the wilderness. Other times huge search parties have been sent out to look for "lost people" who have returned to civilization but neglected to notify anyone.

A fragmented team inevitably becomes a weaker team, especially if the skill level and group equipment is unevenly distributed. Breaking up the group ahead of time into self-sustaining units can mitigate this problem but will also lessen the incentive to stay together. A possible solution is to carry two-way radios. The most effective solution is to have a leader who can control the group, sets a reasonable pace, and does not always lead from the front.

9.14 Disappearing trail

You're hiking on a trail that disappears and reappears with irritating regularity.

This often occurs when traveling on animal trails or trails that run through different types of terrain. A trail may be well defined through the trees but disappear completely when crossing a boulder field, only to reappear at the next patch of trees. Sometimes a trail simply ends. In moderate, open terrain you may choose to ignore the trail and simply travel in the correct general direction. Trails generally follow the path of least resistance so choosing an off-trail route that minimizes hardship will increase your chances of stumbling onto a trail if it exists. Keep in mind that most animal trails eventually lead to water and almost always lead to a pass if there is one ahead. In addition, some animals are experts at creating trails that contour across slopes.

One thing you want to avoid is paralleling a perfectly good trail for long distances. It may be prudent to zigzag your way forward if you're reasonably certain that there is a trail nearby. If the terrain is too rough or the vegetation too thick for reasonable off-trail travel, you may be forced to waste a lot of time looking for the trail. Once you find the trail, pay close attention to every detail in your surroundings to avoid losing it.

9.15 Whiteout

A fog bank rolls in and it starts snowing as you ski across a large, snow-covered ice field, creating a condition known as a whiteout. Nevertheless, you decide that there is enough visibility to continue. After an hour of navigating by instinct, you come across a pair of tracks, and realize that these are your own tracks.

A whiteout doesn't necessarily imply that you can't see anything. It means that you cannot distinguish between things that are white. Brightly colored or dark objects can often be seen from some distance away. On the other hand, snow-covered ground blends in with the fog and it's very difficult or impossible to assess the shape of the surrounding terrain. Distance and depth perception are distorted. Travel can be treacherous because crevasses or snow-covered cliff edges are often invisible, even if they are just one step away.

Successful navigation in whiteout conditions requires faith in your instruments. Without a compass, most people end up traveling the path of least resistance, downhill and with the wind. If the terrain is flat and there is no wind, most people will travel around in circles. A map, compass, and altimeter or GPS receiver is essential. Use your altimeter or GPS receiver to pinpoint your position on the map, and then take a compass bearing toward an intermediate target along your route. If you just have a map and compass, do a rough estimate of your position and then take a bearing toward a large target. Move extremely slowly as you follow the compass bearing. Ignore your directional instincts. If you're unsure of how steep the slope is ahead, test the slope by throwing rocks or snowballs in front of you.

Moving in a straight line in a whiteout is very difficult, even with a compass. If you're traveling solo, look at the compass every few steps to stay on track and take frequent back bearings. If the back bearing doesn't point directly toward your tracks, move sideways until it does. If you're part of a group, travel in a file with the last person carrying the compass and the first person acting as a reference point. The last person checks the compass bearing and periodically directs the first person to veer left or right.

Do not underestimate the inherent dangers of traveling in a whiteout. Unless there is an urgent need to continue or you're certain there is no dangerous terrain ahead, stop until the visibility improves. If you decide to move, take appropriate measures such as roping up to reduce the risks.

9.16 Trail from lake

You drag a canoe down a trail through deep forest to a lake. After reaching the shoreline, you paddle to the other end of the lake for an overnight stay. On your return, you cannot find the trail that you used the previous day. The shoreline looks the same everywhere and the trailhead is hidden from view by trees.

All of these bays look the same

On your outgoing journey, you were moving toward the lake, a large catching feature that was almost impossible to miss. On your return, you're faced with the reverse situation, trying to find a small target, the trailhead, from an indistinguishable location on a large feature. The trailhead is a critical location that you must mark on your outward journey. You could mark it as a GPS waypoint or by recording a triangulation bearing. Only one bearing is needed because the shoreline is a linear feature. If you don't have any navigation equipment, mark the trailhead with flagging tape, or build a rock cairn or a branch tripod before setting off. Also, note any shoreline catching features that would let you know that you've paddled past the trailhead.

Having failed to mark the trailhead, you are faced with a potentially long and tedious scouting expedition. Start from a point well back from where you think the trailhead is located and slowly paddle forward along the shoreline while keeping your eyes glued for any signs of the trail. If anything looks promising, go ashore to check it out.

9.17 No GPS signal

On your quest to conquer Mount McKinley, you decide to climb the avalanche-prone, north-facing Wickersham Wall. After a week of climbing and acclimatizing, you pull out your GPS receiver from the bottom of your pack to check your altitude. For some reason, your receiver refuses to get a position fix.

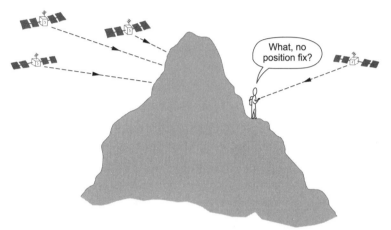

The orbits of GPS satellites carry them to a maximum latitude of about 55°N. Because Mount McKinley is at a latitude of about 63°N, most satellites that are visible from the north-facing Wickersham Wall are the ones that happen to be in northern positions on the opposite side of Earth. The great orbital heights of the satellites allow position fixes even at high latitudes. In fact, your GPS receiver can get an accurate fix at the geographic poles. The problem arises when a mountain or other obstacle blocks a significant portion of the sky and the rest of the sky doesn't have enough satellites for a position fix. This commonly occurs on steep, north faces in the northern hemisphere, and steep, south faces in the southern hemisphere, particularly at high latitudes.

You may eventually get a position fix if you leave your GPS receiver switched on long enough. The satellites are constantly moving and a favorable configuration may temporarily appear.

It is always a good idea to bring along an altimeter when climbing steep walls where knowing your elevation is often more important than knowing your horizontal position. If the visibility permits, try triangulating your horizontal position with a compass. Be aware that a slight horizontal error on a steep slope will translate into a large elevation error on the map.

If you brought along a suitable thermometer, you could measure the temperature of boiling water, and then estimate your elevation based on this temperature. The boiling temperature of pure water is 100 °C at sea level, and decreases by 1 °C for every 300 m of elevation gain (Section 6.6). For example, if your boiling temperature is 84 °C, your elevation would be (100 - 84) x 300 m = 4800 m.

9.18 Back roads

Walking along an abandoned logging road, you're unable to find the fork of a branch road that is clearly marked on your map. To confirm your position, you take a GPS position fix, then an altimeter reading, and finally use compass triangulation. All methods put you at the same location on the map near the road fork, but after a thorough search of the area, you cannot find the branch road.

This is a situation where you should seriously question the accuracy of your map. Like other navigational tools, maps cannot always be trusted. Even high-quality maps from reputable mapmakers are prone to errors, especially regarding man-made features such as roads.

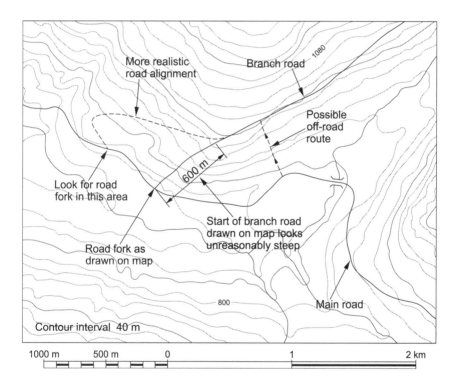

By carefully analyzing the contour lines on the map, you will notice that the branch road starts out with a very steep hill. Over a distance of 600 m, the road rises about 7 contour lines for an elevation gain of 280 m. This works out to a gradient of 47% or a slope angle of 25°, much too steep for a drivable road. Since it is unlikely that the mapmaker drew in a road that never existed, look at the adjacent contour lines for an alternate road alignment that makes sense.

You will discover that the slope eases a few hundred meters to the northwest. Scout out this area for a possible start of the branch road. If you don't find the branch road there, investigate other reasonable possibilities. If this fails, travel off-road toward your destination. You may eventually stumble onto the road if you choose a route that intersects a reasonable road alignment.

Logging and mining roads are often temporary features that may or may not have been drawn on your map. They can evolve into a web of roads that end abruptly. Getting lost on back roads is actually much more common than getting lost in true wilderness areas. It is often difficult to know if you're on the correct road until you've traveled along that road for some distance. Survey the surrounding terrain as you travel to keep track of your position, and use a compass to ensure that you are moving in the correct general direction. Don't be afraid to pull out your altimeter or GPS receiver if you are uncertain of your position.

9.19 Food stash

For a long ski traverse, you decide to hire a ski plane to place a food stash on a glacier near the midpoint of your route. You accompany the pilot when the stash is dropped and plant a wand in the middle of the stash. You then use your compass to triangulate the position of the stash, dutifully recording the field bearings to the landmarks. Unfortunately, all the landmarks are hidden by fog when you reach the vicinity of the stash during your traverse, preventing you from triangulating your position.

Given the importance of finding the stash, you should employ several backup methods to mark its location. Options include marking the stash's location as a GPS waypoint or an altimeter reading. An effective method for zeroing-in on a buried stash is to place an avalanche transceiver inside the stash. Don't forget to insert a fresh set of batteries and make sure the unit is switched on. You will need a second transceiver to find the stash.

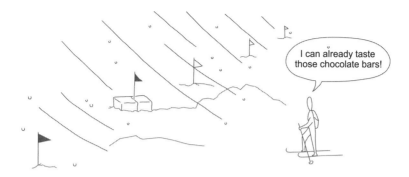

A reliable method for marking a stash is to plant a series of wands, about 50 m apart, on both sides of the stash. The line of wands should be perpendicular to your expected direction of travel, with the stash at the center. Placing different colored wands on each side of the stash and numbering them according to their distance from the stash will make the stash even easier to find. Be aware that wands often melt out and fall down or get completely covered by new snow. Make sure the wands are long enough to be planted deep into the snow and still stick up high above the snow.

9.20 Antarctic ordeal

During his ill-fated Antarctic expedition from 1914 to 1916, Ernest Shackleton's ship was trapped by ice for 9 months, and then crushed by the ice. He and his crew abandoned the ship and then drifted on the pack ice for 5 months to open water. With three lifeboats, they managed to reach uninhabited Elephant Island just off the Antarctic Peninsula.

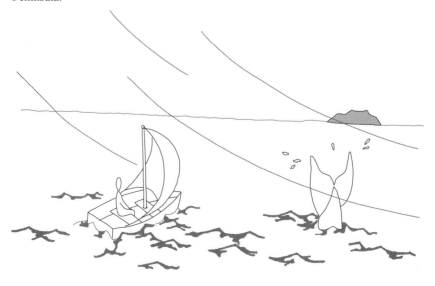

To get help, Shackleton and five other men set sail in one of the small boats toward South Georgia, 1300 km away. It would be a onetime opportunity. If their course was off by more than a few degrees, the boat would miss the island and disappear into the South Atlantic where they would surely perish. The available navigation tools were a compass, sextant, chronometer, nautical almanac, and pen and paper.

Shackleton's navigator, Frank Worsley, plotted a course to South Georgia, taking into account the prevailing winds and currents. During the 16-day voyage, the skies were mostly overcast and the boat was continually pounded by enormous waves and gale force winds. On the wildly pitching boat, Worsley managed to take only four sextant sights of the sun between thick clouds. The location of the horizon could only be guessed because of the poor visibility. After taking the sights, Worsley consulted the soggy almanac and used a pencil to do the calculations. The rest of the navigating was done solely by dead reckoning. The boat miraculously followed a near perfect course to South Georgia and the whole expedition team was eventually rescued. Some people regard this event as one of the greatest feats in navigation history.

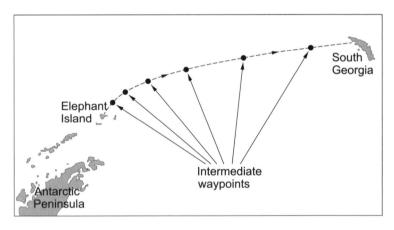

Trying to recreate this journey today using a GPS receiver instead of a sextant would make the navigation a lot easier, but plotting the proper course would be just as difficult. Marking the position of South Georgia as a waypoint in your receiver and following a great circle route to the island would not work because winds and currents would push you off course. Instead, you would have to follow a route consisting of a series of intermediate waypoints that take into account expected currents and winds as well as how fast your boat can move relative to the water.

Frank Worsley was obviously gifted but still required years of practice as a ship navigator to perfect his navigation skills. Today's aspiring navigator should take note. High-tech gadgets are no substitute for practical experience and clear, rational thinking.

9.21 Polynesian journey

In 1976, a replica Polynesian, doubled-hulled, ocean-going canoe set sail from Maui (20°53'N, 156°41'W) to Tahiti (17°33'S, 149°36'W). Only traditional South Pacific navigation techniques were to be used on this voyage that covered a straight-line distance of around 4300 km, mostly across open ocean. No navigation instruments were carried onboard. The crew included expert Micronesian navigator Mau Piailug.

Before taking off, Piailug selected a proposed route, taking into account factors such as prevailing winds and currents, expected weather for the season, availability of convenient astronomical bodies, and the capability of the vessel. He also established alternate routes in case things didn't work out as planned. The vessel first sailed northeast, which was deliberately in the wrong direction. This was done to sail as far east as possible before losing sight of the Hawaiian Islands. The navigation was done by terrain association on this section of the voyage, using the islands as landmarks. After skirting around the Big Island, the course was set to the southeast, in the direction where the star Antares rises. This deliberate eastward offset was to compensate for strong, west-flowing ocean currents.

As the vessel moved southward, the height of Polaris above the horizon was used to estimate the latitude while Piailug used dead reckoning to estimate the longitude. He calculated the speed of the boat by looking at how fast the water flowed past the hull and used patterns of ocean swells to keep the vessel pointed in the right direction during periods of cloud cover. Every slight change in wind direction was noted. Between latitudes 8°N and 4°N, the crew encountered the doldrums, a region of weak and unpredictable winds. The vessel made slow southerly progress during this portion of the voyage, but was thankfully pushed eastward about 200 km by east-flowing currents.

The crew inferred that they had crossed the equator shortly after seeing Polaris very low on the horizon. From here, the course was set toward the Southern Cross when it was halfway up its maximum height above the horizon. This bearing, equivalent to south-southeast, was calculated to compensate for west-flowing currents. This bearing would also direct the vessel toward the Tuamotu Archipelago, a target several hundred kilometers wide. Zenith stars were used to calculate the latitude. At one point, Spica passed almost straight overhead putting the vessel at about 11°30'S, and later Zubenelgenubi put their latitude at 15°S.

Unfortunately, the southeast trade winds were too southerly that year and could not compensate for the westerly current. Piailug had a backup plan in case the westward drift caused the boat to miss the Tuamotu Archipelago. Instead of trying to directly find a small target like Tahiti, he would sail northeast against the current to approach the Tuamotu Archipelago from the southwest. After reaching and identifying one of the islands, he would know the boat's exact location and could then sail straight for Tahiti. This plan was not needed because the familiar swells from the southeast abruptly stopped and a crewmember noticed a couple of terns that normally don't venture more than 50 km from land. This could only mean they were very close to land. A short time later, the crew spotted Mataiva, the westernmost island of the Tuamotu Archipelago. From here, Tahiti was an easy navigation target with cloud formations above its mountains visible far out to sea.

Since then, several other long, open ocean voyages have been successfully completed without any navigation instruments. This type of navigation requires years of practice and is not an exact science. Your presumed position could be off by several hundred kilometers. It does however teach an important lesson. The world is filled with navigational clues that can be exploited by a skilled navigator.

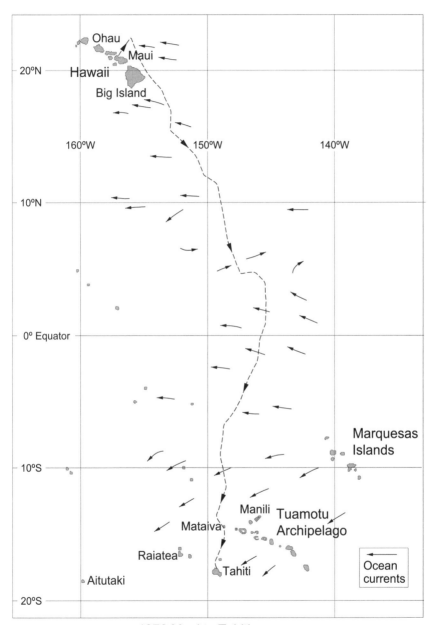

1976 Maui to Tahiti voyage

Index

Index